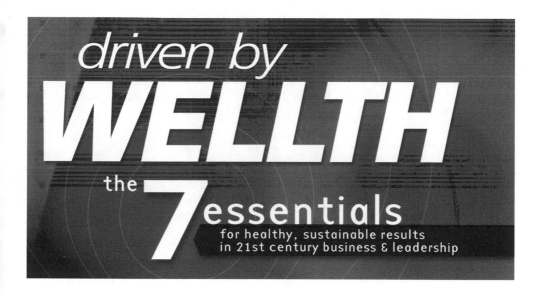

driven by WELLTH
the 7 essentials
for healthy, sustainable results
in 21st century business & leadership

Julie **Maloney** ■ Renee **Moorefield, Ph.D.**

wellth
productions

Boulder, Colorado, USA

Driven By Wellth

Copyright © 2004 by Julie Maloney, Renee Moorefield.
P.O. Box 19406, Boulder, CO 80308-2406
www.wellthproductions.com

Published by Wellth Productions, P.O. Box 19406, Boulder, CO 80308-2406

Driven By Wellth
Julie Maloney, Renee Moorefield, Ph.D.

Cover and interior design by idesignetc

Cataloging-in-Publication Data is on file with the Library of Congress.
(Provided by Quality Books, inc.)

Maloney, Julie, 1964-
    Driven by wellth : the 7 essentials for healthy,
sustainable results in 21st century business and
leadership / Julie Maloney and Renee Moorefied.
    p. cm.
    Includes bibliographical references
    LCCN 2003116764
    ISBN 0-9747746-7-7

    1. Leadership—Moral and ethical aspects. 2. Social
responsibility of business. 3. Success in business.
I. Moorefield, Renee. II. Title.

HD57.7.M355 2004   658.4'092
                        QBI04-200010

Printed and bound in the United States of America

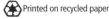Printed on recycled paper

The research that supports *Driven by Wellth* will be updated periodically. Sign up for a FREE electronic version of these updates at www.wellthproductions.com.

For purchasing bulk orders of *Driven by Wellth*, call 303.772.9000.

Endorsements

In today's world, corporations are affecting not only every aspect of our personal lives but also the fabric of life itself at a planetary scale. In this new context, leadership must be thought of from a new value system able to embrace this higher level of complexity. Julie Maloney and Renee Moorefield in this wonderful book contribute generously to the birthing of this new thinking. They also give us guidance to design new steps in the praxis of a new brand of leading. What a joy to read it!

Julio Olalla, President, The Newfield Network, Inc., Coaching School and Consulting Company

Driven by Wellth offers great practical, healthy and spiritual abundance to those who have the wisdom to follow *The 7 Essentials*sm. It is critical that industrial leaders take advantage of this information to preserve the best of modern technology and the future of civilization. I highly recommend it!

C. Norman Shealy, M.D., Ph.D., President, Holos University Graduate Seminary, Founding President, American Holistic Medical Association, Author of 21 books and over 290 scientific publications, including *Sacred Healing* and *90 Days to Stress-Free Living*

*The 7 Essentials*sm framework developed by Moorefield and Maloney gives business leaders a practical roadmap to align your actions and thoughts—at home, at work and in the world—with the person you are deep down inside. That process of self-discovery through *The 7 Essentials*sm can open new paths to greater health, performance and possibilities for achievement as a new kind of leader for the 21st century, one driven and surrounded by wellth from the inside out.

Linda Distlerath, Vice President, Global Health Policy, Merck & Co., Inc.

New challenges bring new opportunities, and today's ever-changing world is ripe with possibility. But unless we are willing to let go of outdated ways of thinking and acting, we're likely to remain spectators as others capitalize on the promise of the future. *Driven by Wellth* brings together a critical set of tools and perspectives to help us create profoundly different ways of living, working and leading in a time of social, economic and ecological upheaval. By learning to value and create health and sustainability in all of our endeavors, we can become more effective leaders and better citizens of the world. Thank you, Julie and Renee, for pointing to a new path forward and providing us with such a handy map to follow!

Janice Molloy, Managing Editor, *The Systems Thinker*

Business, like no other sector in our society, has such transformative potential. Renee Moorefield and Julie Maloney write, beautifully, about what it means to create a community of people who can add value to the planet, or not. Their map to the future, for me, is incredibly compelling.

Kim Jordan, CEO, New Belgium Brewery

In the crowded field of books on leadership, Maloney and Moorefield stand out because they offer ideas, inspiration and practical tools for achieving results—an increasingly difficult challenge in today's rapidly changing and hectic world. After reading *Driven by Wellth*, leaders know better ways to navigate through the ambiguity of the future.

Steffie Allen, President, Athena Group

Maloney and Moorefield's book is so compelling, uplifting and provocative. It will change the way we think about leadership, and will force us to be more conscious and mindful about our choices and actions. *Driven by Wellth* offers a framework for making decisions—they call it *'The 7 Essentials^sm'*—and it's a blend of science, philosophy, spirituality, wisdom and sound thinking. This book should be required reading for emerging and veteran leaders, alike.

Kathy Simon, Director, Robert H. and Beverly A. Deming Center
for Entrepreneurship, University of Colorado

After decades of working with individual clients and global businesses worldwide, I know that leaders everywhere are called to play a much bigger game in order to create the best for the world, for their organizations and for their personal lives. *Driven by Wellth* provides leaders the inspiration and tools for stepping up to this bigger game with powerful, creative and holistic decisions.

Laura Whitworth, CPCC & MCC, and former CPA, co-founder of
The Bigger Game Company, The Coaches Training Institute
and Co-Active Space Leadership Program
and an author of the popular book *Co-Active Coaching*

Having first heard Renee Moorefield and Julie Maloney speak at the Lifestyles of Health and Sustainability Conference in Colorado, I was immediately struck by their level of clarity, integrity and drive in the area of sustainable business. Their strength is in helping companies create an environment that is balanced, inspirational and motivating. Health is "Wellth" in my industry, and Wisdom Works and *Driven by Wellth* have both been instrumental in helping me define and clarify my goals so I can continue to create a healthy, sustainable and economically sound company I am proud of.

Jennifer Workman, M.S., R.D. Founder of The Balanced Approach® Nutrition/Weight
Management Program, specializing in Sports, Medical, Integrative & Ayurvedic nutrition,
and author of the book *Stop Your Cravings*

The boys were in bed, Tam was reading, and throughout the quiet evening of pondering wellth, I found a peaceful, reaffirming sense of what I knew I was doing right, with the anticipation of wanting to bring the tools outlined by the book to a particularly difficult design project. The book provides a wonderful, thoughtful, insightful guide to let me see me and those I work with, both co-workers and clients, in a way that can let me be a more thoughtful, insightful leader. Thinking through my next steps on the project, it is already headed in a better direction. What a gift to the world *Driven by Wellth* is. Thank you for your work.

Morey Bean, Partner, Colorado Architecture Partnership, LLP,
and also 1999 Colorado Architect of the Year

Driven by Wellth is a must-read for anyone who is mindful about the way business practices should, can and must be conducted in today's global workplace. The ideas brought forth by Maloney and Moorefield are insightful, applicable and timely. As a CEO of a national organic foods restaurant company, I'm proud of the many socially responsible endeavors we endorse, and am grateful for this revolutionary book that serves up a why-do and how-to manual. *Driven by Wellth* will encourage all of us business leaders to continue on the path of authenticity, and challenge us to simultaneously raise the bar, while heightening the awareness as to what constitutes sustainable success.

Lauren Bell, CEO and Founder, Wild Sage Foods, Inc.,
"Changing the World—One Bite Atta Time"

If you notice that you spend more time lately reflecting upon the mission of your work. . . the mission of your life . . . and find yourself faced with the thought provoking and heart provoking question "For the sake of what?", this book is for you.

Chris Trani, Leadership & Communication Coach, Janus Capital Management

Driven by Wellth provides elegant, powerful and simple ideas and tools for finding direction. It is just what the 21st century business world needs right now.

Pat Barlow, VP of Human Resources, Europe, Middle East, Africa, Merck and Co., Inc.

This is a book whose time has come! *Driven by Wellth* is essential reading for exploring the converging forces of social change that will impact business. It will benefit anyone who is interested in a more holistic approach to business based on satisfying the emotional, moral, psychological, humanitarian and intellectual needs of people—an approach that will attract and keep energized, high performing, creative workers. When we are able to break out of the narrow set of values that have become our ultimate ambition—inauthentic values by which "success" is currently defined—we will open a floodgate of wellth and possibility.

Joan Boykin, Director of PR, Hain Celestial

The 7 Essentials[sm] framework provides both the analytical and reflective tools that 21st century business leaders need in order to engage today's complex challenges as opportunities to build new models of success that will lead to a healthier global society.

Mark Wilding, Director, Naropa University's Marpa Center for Business and Economics

The world is in great need of a shift in attitudes and values. Maloney and Moorefield offer a guide with which to create new aspirations for 21st century leaders. Their framework, *The 7 Essentials*[sm], provides a new way of thinking and being that will change how business is done.

Michael Serino, Senior Director, Executive Development, Merck & Co., Inc.

Table of Contents

Acknowledgments

Long ago, someone told us that writing a book is a community affair. This book would not have come into being without significant efforts of a group of people, all of whom have vastly different talents yet share the same underlying aspiration: *to promote the values and practices of healthier forms of success within life, leadership, business and society.* We are grateful to the genius and the immense spirit that each person brought to *Driven by Wellth.*

First, we extend many thanks to our clients for their higher aspirations and courage. It is a privilege to partner with you, in service of the visions you dare to dream and pursue against all odds. You set new heights for 21st century leaders and companies everywhere, and you've been a source of inspiration to complete *Driven by Wellth.*

For reviewing our work and providing invaluable feedback along the way, many thanks go to Jane Cocking, Dianne Culhane, Wanda Gentile, Barb Lawton, Bill Marino, Micki McMillan-Blacker, Bill Montague, Nina Peterson, Susan Rissman and Michael Serino. Your honest critiques made a big difference.

For applying our holistic decision-making framework within your life and work, and for being a community within which we could explore the values of health and sustainability more deeply, thank you, Wisdom Partners, a growing group of professional leadership coaches and trainers. Dana Blalock, Nicki Carpenter, Jane Cocking, Dianne Culhane, Peg Long, James Macsay, LeeAnn Mallory, Micki McMillan-Blacker, Nina Peterson, Gail Rucker and Scott Spann, you are exceptional people, and we appreciate your support.

For providing research, editing and publishing support, we wholeheartedly thank Kim Arbuckle, Karen Artl, Mark Bowers, Tabitha Brown, Nicki Hagge, Micki McMillan-Blacker, Nina Peterson, Alison Samter, Dana Sherrer and Keith Sherrer. You helped turn a rambling of ideas into a book of which we are proud.

When an author is trying to transform ideas into reality, thank goodness there's enlightened guidance available. For us, that guidance came in the form of Monte Unger. Thank you, Monte, not only for being a superb writing coach and editor, but also for your continued optimism and encouragement. You are truly a reminder of our larger spiritual purpose in the world.

Along the way, we had a few cheerleaders! These people frequently asked how the book was coming along (and really wanted to know). And, they provided an enthusiastic 'You can do it!' just when we needed to hear it. A huge thanks to Kim Arbuckle, Sally Archuleta, John Buck, Micki McMillan-Blacker, Wanda Gentile, Pam Jones, Tommy Patin, Nina Peterson, Susan Rissman, Melinda Treml and Kelly Young for helping us stay focused on realizing this dream.

We are blessed with wonderful husbands and families, the foundation and meaning behind all that we do. Thank you Kevin, David, Caitlin, Jillian, Silvie (okay, she's a dog, but a key family member!), Marge, Bob, Nancy, Tommy, John and Becky as well as our siblings and extended families. All of you make life and work richer, healthier and happier. We are incredibly thankful for you.

We've also learned that family isn't always a blood relation. Family means the person to which you commit yourself. It means seeing the grace that is the other person even when they don't see that in themselves. Family means persevering through thick and thin because you value the relationship. It means partnering and learning together. Therefore, we wholeheartedly acknowledge each other and the shared paths we've traveled, whether through authoring this book, building a sustainable company, doing work with clients, going on long hikes and vacations, or having heartfelt conversations over many years. Our friendship is a blessing.

Finally, we are deeply appreciative of the grander creative force that founds and evolves all of life itself. Learning how to collaborate with this force is the essence of this book.

Julie Maloney and Renee Moorefield, Ph.D.
December 2003

Dedication

This book is dedicated to 21st century leaders everywhere who strive to
make a difference in the health and sustainability of people's lives, companies
and civilization. Your real-life stories, sincere aspirations and commitment
to positive change inspired this book. May you continue to encourage and
accelerate the growing, generative movement toward a radically better world.
We are grateful for the ways you demonstrate courage, compassion and
wisdom in leadership every day.

Foreword

Dianne Marie Culhane
Director, The Coca-Cola Company

I don't believe there was a specific moment when I suddenly realized we need a *different kind of leadership*. It was more of an evolving awareness, beginning as a gnawing sense, an intuition, that something didn't feel natural and that there had to be a better way.

I got that sense as I noticed more and more of my colleagues working harder and harder, in the process sacrificing their health, losing weight (or gaining it!) and losing relationships, only to find their sacrifice rewarded with more pressure and more crises.

The feeling nagged at me more as I watched different leaders in similar positions responding to powerful structures they couldn't see, making the same mistakes over and over again, based on a collectively held and unchallenged view of their world.

The feeling grew to a kind of incredulous disbelief as I witnessed that innovations with the potential for dramatic change were carelessly discarded by those in charge simply because they weren't "invented here."

And even before the headlines began revealing the litany of horrors in the corporate "crisis of trust," I had become deeply sensitive to a growing population of employees and consumers that wanted—demanded—a new breed of leadership; leadership that is responsible, authentic, holistic…but also able to deliver business results.

Much has been said about the dramatic and changing environment in which we find ourselves. Every one of us, every day, can bear testament to the new technologies, new ways of thinking, new demands and new opportunities that are hallmarks of this "new world of work." We know it's true, not because the *Wall Street Journal* reports it is so, but because we're feeling its effects at this very moment.

And yet, amidst the opportunity and the anxiety remains a persistent ambiguity around what needs to be done. When faced with a burning platform, our instinct for self-preservation entices us to leap blindly into the smoke. But such a reactive stance only removes us from the thing we don't want; it fails to produce anything *new*. What is missing for many leaders is the destination; a vision for a better alternative, where results are achieved and sustained in ways that generate health for the business, for the people inside, for the markets... and, indeed, for the planet.

Some themes about this new model of leadership are emerging. If you make a habit of scanning the business bestsellers, you may have noticed a change in the tone and content of the leadership literature within the past few years. The language has evolved beyond the "get it done" kinds of rhetoric to include a sensitivity that wasn't present even in the early 90s; the idea that "HOW leaders deliver results is as important as the results themselves." (And, furthermore, the "how" actually impacts the results themselves.) The discussion is becoming palpably more humanistic and holistic. A lot of ideas are entering the popular thinking on leadership that once lived an isolated existence in their disparate worlds of philosophy, theology, sociology and even the biological sciences. But like the markets themselves, the walls that separate ideas have come down.

It is a critical time to talk about leadership. As a new way of thinking enters the public discourse, there is much at stake. This is more than the evolution of a business model; the health of the planet hangs in the balance. Traditional reductionist thinking puts business results at odds with the possibility of a healthier and happier planet. But the two goals are more profoundly compatible than many recognize.

The ideas in *Driven by Wellth* resonate with me. The authors share a basic belief that I hold dearly, a belief that is potent in today's crisis of cynicism. It is the belief that organizations are, at their core, noble structures that can validate and nurture the universal hunger for aspiration, wholeness and achievement. Consider: Business is the place where every day we do not simply tolerate but embrace differences for the purpose of creating new possibility. It is the place where doors are opened, countries are joined and economies are enriched. And it is the place where human beings are given the resources to grow, learn and contribute to a vast, multi-cultural web of opportunity.

The central question of *Driven by Wellth* is both simple and profound: *How can success be achieved and sustained in a healthy manner?* The "healthy manner" is the clincher here, and the authors, Julie Maloney and Renee Moorefield, rise to the challenge with "*The 7 Essentials^{sm}*" framework—a brilliant integration of ageless wisdom from multiple disciplines.

The 7 Essentials^sm draws from the study of *organic systems*, including living systems theories from the East and West, complexity science and systems thinking.

That's just the beginning. From the realm of *human systems*, you will encounter fundamentals of the psychology of ultimate concerns, wellness, organizational learning, constructivism, religious thought, integral theory and others.

And from *marketplace theory*, you may recognize elements of creative capital theory, eco-economics and natural or restorative capitalism, and more.

Yes, it's all in here, and the authors distill it all with far more simplicity and flair than you might have thought possible. (On second thought, if you share their conviction that *it's all connected*, then it seems perfectly natural.) What is amazing about *Driven by Wellth* is that Maloney and Moorefield present it in a crystal-clear framework, always with an emphasis on practical application.

But most of all, it has the courage to speak to the desires of all human beings for health, wealth and happiness—in themselves, in their relationships and in their organizations. It is this pursuit that will characterize the 21st century leader.

The possibility of a world that is healthier truly lies within our hands. Enormous leverage lies in the transformation of our own organizations and our own leadership. Let Julie Maloney and Renee Moorefield illuminate your way to a new destination, one that leads to health, creativity, aspiration, endless possibilities and concrete, performance-driven results.

Dianne Marie Culhane
Director, Company Image Communications
Worldwide Public Affairs and Communications
The Coca-Cola Company

October, 2003

the evolutionary leap

"We are living in the greatest revolution in history—a huge spontaneous upheaval of the entire human race: not the revolution planned and carried out by any particular party, race, or nation, but a deep elemental boiling over of all the inner contradictions that have ever been in man, a revelation of the chaotic forces inside everybody. This in not something we have chosen, nor is it something we are free to avoid." [1]

Thomas Merton, Christian contemplative

"Is life really a game of just survival? Must dog eat dog? Can there be no meaning beyond making money and acquiring power, both of which can be lost in a heartbeat? Is there a way that matters by which I can contribute, not just to my family, but to my neighbors, the truly disadvantaged, my peers, my country—the global village?

A growing number of business people have begun answering these questions in an altruistic manner. No longer is their goal solely to look out for number one—themselves—but now, it's also to contribute to the greater good in a particularly novel way—through their business practices." [2]

Daryl Paulson, author and CEO, BioScience Laboratories, Inc.

---

the evolutionary leap

the birth of a new set of values to navigate the challenges
of the 21st century

We live in complex times. As business leaders, we're overrun with
a staggering amount of decisions to make every day, choices that affect the
future of our companies, whole cultures and our daily lives.

We must continually invent new products, services and, often, entire
markets, but privately we long to lean on what worked in the past. We feel
pressured to immediately answer Wall Street with increased stock value, yet
our gut tells us to keep an eye on our company's fitness for the long haul.
We try to stay focused on the business of doing business, but we can only
do so by navigating difficult social issues. Likewise, we want to improve our
personal health and our relationships, yet we struggle with the weight of
work on our shoulders.

Every moment seems like a compromise, a juggling act, a constant 'give
and take,' and it appears there's no end in sight.

To make matters worse, no one else has definitive, sustainable solutions
to our most pressing business conundrums. It seems like no other company
or leader really knows how to make decisions any better than we do. We
have to figure things out for ourselves.

We didn't ask for the predicaments we face, and we surely didn't
intentionally create them. What's more, we genuinely don't want to reproduce
our problems over and over again. It seems too easy to be sucked into the
latest crisis or robotically follow the downward spiral of others. The stark truth
is that the world is fundamentally rearranging itself right before our eyes, and
we can't handle it using the same old approaches we've used in the past.

In business, society and our personal lives, we find ourselves thrown into a period in the evolution of our leadership where we are called to discover a fundamentally new way to see our problems, a new way to make decisions, a new way to relate to one another and a new way to guide our businesses and our lives. The complex challenges we face are insisting that we cultivate a *new set of values* to advance healthier forms of success than we've known how to produce before.

However, to operate from a healthier set of values first requires that we take a hard, honest look at the values we're using right now.

A Modern Set of Values Guides Our Progress

For the past few hundred years, a dominant set of values has guided practically every arena of society, especially business. Mass production, standardization, convenience, the work ethic, globalization, scientific breakthroughs and technological advancement are a few of the values that have ruled our attention. In this modern value set, *short-term profit* has been the definite frontrunner leading the values pack, endorsed by a Western culture that heralds economic growth as king.

In fact, we've created entire business and organizing models in order to pursue our modern values for their own sake. The modern value set has been the looking glass through which we've led organizations, harnessed resources (like people and money) and measured the worth of our achievements and our lives.

We've distinguished our modern values as a sign of progress. Due to our values, we've made some improvements in how we manage the intricacies of business and society as well as how we regard humanity. Today, more people have access to revolutionary medical innovations, like organ transplants, blockbuster drugs and the latest disease research. More people use communication technologies, like wireless cell phones and the Internet, which shrink cultural and geographic barriers worldwide. Plus, more people are connected to a diversity of ideas and customs with which to make better choices for their careers, their lifestyles and their spiritual journeys. Guided by our modern value set, we believe we've become more efficient, advanced and humane.

The Same Modern Values Cause Us Problems

Even with the progress we've enjoyed, however, our prevailing modern values aren't working for us anymore, at least, not by themselves. It's not that motives such as money and globalization are bad. Not at all. It's that we've come to idolize these values to the disregard of everything else.

At our worst, we've reduced business and leadership decisions to a simple mantra...

- Make a profit ...however you can.

- Do it quick.

- The more, the better.

Too commonly, we take action as if profit-centric values are the only conduit to success rather than questioning whether or not these values actually give us the quality of life and livelihood we've collectively worked so hard to achieve.

No wonder we've lost touch with the larger costs we're causing society, nature, our corporations and our selves. Our modern value system is a driving thrust, so hidden in our psyche and entrenched in our institutions, that we aren't forced to think about the consequences of our actions. Thinking about the consequences goes directly against the grain of what our values reward. Sadly, to satisfy our ambition for profit, we override our better judgment on too many occasions.

Nowhere are our profit-seeking values more worshipped than in business. Paradoxically, we are realizing that the same values we've used for decades to manage our company now interfere with its performance. Take, for example, executives who measure success or failure exclusively on their company's quarterly stock price. For these leaders, any strategy, whether massive lay-offs or foolish business deals, is rational and justifiable as long as it produces quick financial gains. Yet, these executives usually fail to build resilient companies that steadfastly weather upset and make money over the long haul.[3] As told daily in news stories like Enron and WorldCom, untold damage to society also materializes through executive short-sightedness.

In defense of purely profit-driven business strategies, some leaders claim, "But we only offer this product because the market demands it!" That kind of response suggests that corporations are passive, merely reacting to the whims of their consumers. Not so. Companies are active agents of change; they use public forums, media and marketing campaigns to bias consumer demand, create new desires within people for products and services and sway the attitudes of entire communities. Business is far from submissive. In fact, among the world's 100 largest economies (such as companies and nations) that influence our cultures and our lives, 51 are corporations.[4] Corporations are dynamic, self-determining and formative forces, accountable to the health of themselves, their marketplace and society as a whole.

As leaders we must wonder what results we really produce with the incredible powers of business under our charge. When we reflect on this closely, we find the real crux behind many of our challenges: we've mindlessly allowed a narrow set of values to become our final ambition rather than the instruments we use to create healthier forms of success. As a result, we've inadvertently caused significant problems for business and society to handle.

We've mindlessly allowed a narrow set of values to become our final ambition rather than the instruments we use to create healthier forms of success.

Moreover, the problems we've created are systemic in nature, widespread and convoluted. Our challenges aren't limited to a few flashpoints on our planet; by many measures, we live in an increasingly unhealthy world overall.

For example, preventable lifestyle-related risks and illnesses, such as physical inactivity, high cholesterol and high blood pressure, once the sole burden of wealthy, industrialized countries, have proliferated to developing regions already troubled with poverty and infectious disease.[5] Malnutrition has risen to alarming numbers, yet under strikingly different symptoms; through under- *and* over-consumption worldwide, 170 million severely underweight children exist side by side with 300 million clinically obese adults.[6] By expanding human activities to all points on the globe, we're rapidly pushing whole species toward extinction, literally shrinking the same biological wealth we've relied on since the birth of humankind.[7] Because our most urgent problems are systemic, there's no single person or entity to blame for them; everyone contributes in some way. We only add to our misery by trying to attack these problems with a value system that's incomplete and insufficient to deal with the overwhelming complexity and magnitude with which our problems confront us.

Our values prevent us from seeing how we're an integral factor in causing our predicaments. They also frequently block us from a crucial realization: we are the only path to discovering meaningful, life-enhancing solutions.

We are the only path to discovering meaningful, life-enhancing solutions.

To twist the screws of fate even tighter, we live in a more *connected* world than ever before. Our problems—and our attempts to resolve them—are no longer isolated to one part of the whole, like a single company or locale; they move through the web of connectedness in which our world environment clearly exists.

Connected: A Central Feature of the 21st Century Environment

Most leaders hold idealistic memories of a time when things were simpler and more controlled (and seemingly more controllable). Yet, nowadays our lives and our business activities are actually more *connected* and, as a result, more complicated. We're influenced by ideas, customs, brands and hardships that span the globe. Around the world, we're making indelible impressions on each other, and like an old sweater that stretches out of its original shape, we can never return to the way we were in times past. We're literally evolving into a different world whether we like it or not.

In this different world, time and space take on new meaning. Unlike the business transactions of even a few decades ago, our business exchanges today are virtually borderless. Popular entertainment like MTV, mass marketing of global brands like McDonalds and international travel by air and sea are a few of the forces that bind our lives, our ideologies and our nations together, escalating both innovation and conflict. With one in 12 people worldwide going online every day,[8] many of our closest relationships are people from other cultures that we communicate with by email instead of talking over the fence with our neighbors next door, and this is reinventing our definition of community. Not to mention the massive land-based and mobile phone systems linking us to any one of two billion people internationally in a matter of moments.[9] Through our borderless connections, we make things happen around the globe in seconds where decades ago it might have taken us months or years.

> The rapidly emerging "global brain" is weaving the human family together into a new level and intensity of relationship. The combined power of the computer Internet, television networks, global satellite systems, cellular telephones, fiber optics, and many more devices has created a perceptual framework within which even those who are agrarians or industrialists in their daily work will increasingly orient themselves.[10]

Both the highest of highs and the lowest of lows confirm how local events ripple in an international chain reaction. Take, for instance, the 2001 U.S. terrorist attacks and stock market crashes that triggered a far-reaching economic slump.[11] Similarly, the 2003 war in Iraq provoked, among other things, 30 million citizens from 600 cities across every continent to march for peace, a unified outpouring unmatched in history.[12] We are so intertwined that the world around us often responds to our actions in unprecedented ways, yet most of the time we don't realize this until after the fact. Through our connectedness, our circle of influence has widened.

"Economic power and decision-making are now distributed over a vastly more numerous and diverse population, reducing the odds that a failure in one corner of the economy will drag down others."[16]

In business, we've learned to profit from the sheer scale of our interconnectedness by selling goods and services on every inch of the planet, from talking on a Nokia cell phone in Botswana to drinking a Coke in the heart of Papau, New Guinea. Global trade totaled over $6.2 trillion in goods (such as oil, cars and food) and $1.6 trillion for services (such as freight and travel) in 2002.[13,14] Because of our connectedness, even with the rise of corporate scandals and military action afflicting the same year, we enjoyed a fairly steady global economy.[15]

Nevertheless, we'd be careless and myopic leaders if we took advantage of our global interdependencies without being mindful of the consequences of our business practices. In this different world we're in, mindfulness can make or break business success. Consider that the world's diminishing fresh water supply is no longer just an environmental challenge; it limits the growth of every food and beverage manufacturer, like PepsiCo and Frito-Lay, where water is a main ingredient. The AIDS-related death toll of so many African people isn't only something for humankind to mourn; it shrinks the entire workforce supporting African business activities, like those of DaimlerChrysler, Intel and Nestle, thereby reducing the economic growth and social health of that region. The rampant obesity of many nations around the globe isn't just a health scare; it incites legal action against companies, like Burger King, demonizes the image of corporations and their products, and demands business to account for its role in the problem. Today, every company, large and small, has to deal with some natural or human challenge that they've never had to manage before in order to do business at all.

Whereas in the past we played the game of business for immediate financial gains, progressive business leaders today must be proactive, conscious and accountable to balance economic, ecological and social returns. Whereas in the past we may have concentrated solely on payback to our company, today's leaders must make holistic company decisions that consider the broader effects of their actions. Leadership capabilities that used to be the domain of only so-called green companies are now threshold skills for every organization.

Today's leaders must make holistic company decisions that consider the broader effects of their actions.

With the best of intentions, we frequently *produce* more problems than we resolve. Our world is undergoing the pangs of birthing into something different, yet our approaches for making decisions and leading our organizations haven't quite evolved. The canaries in the coalmine have stopped singing, forewarning us of the penalties for how we use our corporate power. The destructive effects of our inadequacies are headlined daily in poor international relations, strained social systems and workplaces filled with burned-out people. Our modern values, and the behaviors they dictate, don't seem to be getting us out of the complex, interconnected dilemmas in which we live.

Our dilemmas are prodding us to reevaluate and broaden our definitions of success, and to use the power of our enterprises more wisely. However, that requires us to lead from a new set of values altogether.

A New Set of Values is Birthing

Just as our modern value system enabled us to surpass challenges we encountered in times past, a new value system is birthing to effectively deal with the complexities of today. This value system holds within it the seeds of promise for a healthier, more sustainable future.

People from all walks of life—consumers, employees, citizens and leaders alike—see the limitations of our current value set. They realize that many of our modern methods for living, working and running organizations are neither beneficial nor sustainable. But they also know that constructive change won't mean simply changing our behaviors without a deeper shift in attitudes, for that would be scratching the surface. Constructive change will mean catalyzing a healthier set of values from which to function altogether. We must incorporate the best of the capabilities and ideas that previous values have given us *and* stretch our beliefs even further. So, a growing number of people everyday are architecting a wider, more integral worldview from which to orient our activities and our cultures.

This new value set has a few key features:[17,18]

- It views the world as a dynamic living system where everything is connected to everything else and where evolution is not only natural, but is an intelligence with which to collaborate.

- It includes and builds on the values of the past, knowing that every value system plays some useful role in collective human development.

- It transcends previous value systems to focus on promoting greater degrees of health, effectiveness and sustainability that benefit every level of life, such as individuals, organizations, industries and the larger natural and social world.

- It relies on our human capacity to reflect, that is, to notice the consequences of our actions and to alter the course of our future through mindful, holistic and meaningful decisions.

By design, this emerging value set compels us to actively participate in the evolution of our selves and our companies, and to discover the conditions that favor health and effectiveness no matter what our situation. This value system requires us to incorporate a greater degree of consciousness into our plans and activities, and broaden our circle of concern from a self-interested to a life-centric orientation.

From executives and politicians to clergy and consumers, this shift toward life-centric values is persuading people of all kinds to experiment with more creative and compassionate responses to complex business and social challenges. In doing so, they not only personally experience a higher quality of well-being and purpose, but they also become part of a progressive movement to define a healthier global culture.

"... a new global culture and consciousness have taken root and are beginning to grow in the world. This represents a shift in consciousness as distinct and momentous as that which occurred in the transition from the agricultural era to the industrial era roughly three hundred years ago... the most distinctive feature of this emerging era is not technological change, but a change in human consciousness." [19]

This new value set radically redefines our current yardstick of business performance. Financial wealth, innovation, market share and the like are useful but impoverished measures to determine true success. More importantly, these motivations become subservient to a higher ambition: *the generation of a new quality of health and effectiveness for life, a new kind of sustained value, or what we call wellth, in all circumstances.* (You'll learn more about wellth in Chapter 3.)

The life-centric value system being born on a widespread scale is changing the basis from which we perceive and experience reality, how we make decisions and the breadth of aspirations we embrace. It reflects *a shift in consciousness*, remaking the very core of how we live, work and model our organizations.

As a leader in business today, this shift in values is something you can't ignore. It matters to you and your company. Chapter 2 will tell you why.

Chapter Highlights

- *As business leaders, we've allowed a narrow set of values to become our final ambition rather than the instruments we use to create healthier forms of success, now and in the future. As a result, we've inadvertently created significant problems for our companies and society to handle.*

- *Our business world is more interconnected and complex than ever before. Today, commercial success, societal prosperity, ethical management and the use of natural resources are inextricably tied. Because of this, we are compelled to redefine our measures of success.*

- *A new value system is emerging which leaders cannot ignore. This value system favors health, effectiveness and sustainability in all activities, including business. It calls corporate leaders to operate from a life-centric orientation and to incorporate a higher degree of consciousness into their business plans and activities.*

- *21st century leaders who run their companies from this life-centric value system are part of a widening and progressive movement to define a healthier global culture.*

the 21st century leader

"Every significant change, every revolutionary idea, every heartfelt gesture that changes one life or a thousand, was once seen as eccentric. Leaders are few and followers many for a reason: change requires bucking the status quo, and a willingness to be perceived as crazy, dangerous, or ridiculous. Revolutionaries, activists, and change makers of every stripe lead because they cannot follow that with which they do not agree. Or which limits their imaginations. They change the world because their passion and conviction will not allow them not to." [1]

Anita Roddick, Founder, The Body Shop

"We have the right to expect more of ourselves, our institutions, and our cultural life. The resources to make the transformation from our present-day acceptance of the mediocre to future realization of our expectations resides in skillful play with the wildness of our own minds. It is free, and readily available. The energy and discipline to transform that wildness into a glorious imagining of the present moment is the discipline and joy of the creative process." [2]

Peter Coyote, actor and author

"Never before has one generation been given so great an opportunity to live lives of transcendent meaning, to take action that can be of such great benefit to so many over such a long period of time." [3]

Fred Branfman, U.S. Presidential speech writer and advisor

the 21st century leader

emerging new values hold the promise
of a new kind of leadership

A new set of life-centric values is emerging in society. As a business leader, you may want to learn about it fast because these values are causing upheaval in three spheres intimately tied to your company's success: *consumers, workers* and *business.*

- **A new breed of consumer**—the estimated 30 percent of our consumer population who are motivated by issues of health and sustainability, and value progressive leadership in business and society.

- **A new breed of worker**—the free agent employee, contractor and vendor who determine success on their own terms rather than on the goalposts set by organizations with which they work.

- **A new breed of business**—the growing fraternity of companies that realize paving the way for a successful future relies on a healthy society.

These new breeds most likely affect your business success whether you are paying attention to them or keeping your head in the sand. More than ever, the life-centric value system evolving today matters to you because it matters to your company's stakeholders.

A New Breed of Consumer

Jorge roams the aisles of Whole Foods to stock up on groceries for the week.

This grocer, now an international chain, offers locally-grown foods in the most natural state, treats employees as well-rounded human beings, creates a high quality shopping experience and acts as a responsible tenant of the world. The company is concerned about health on every level, from its consumers to employees to planet Earth, and that matters to Jorge. Stopping at the frozen foods, he scans the fat content on a gallon of organic ice cream. He wants to live life to the fullest, and he figures keeping a healthy body and frequenting a healthy grocer will help him do just that.

Jorge is just one of a growing breed of consumers who are designing a better life for themselves through the products, services and companies they choose. Marketplace and sociological studies title this subculture by a variety of names, like the *cultural creatives*[4] and the *LOHAS* (lifestyles of health and sustainability)[5] market. Regardless of the name, the research points to a common thread: an emerging consumer market with a cohesive set of values for a high quality of life, health and work. You may be one of this breed yourself.

"Consuming in the 21st century is a new form of activism."[7]

Gary Hirshberg, CEO, Stonyfield Farms

Beyond making money and acquiring things, people in this subculture are rewriting the scorecard of success. They hold a broader vision for themselves and organizations to include: responsible growth, embracing diversity, human rights, valuing natural resources, fair trade, ethical leadership, meaningful work, personal growth, spiritual evolution and authentic living. Consumers in this subculture reflect over 30 percent of the U.S. market (that's 68 million consumers!), a base that grew 7 percent from 2002 to 2003.[6]

"Once a minimum material sufficiency is secured, national or personal income is not correlated with people's happiness. If we reframe the "more is better" game and focus on maximizing fulfillment rather than disposable income, we will realize the fallacy of confusing quality with quantity of life."[8]

This breed of consumer cuts across a wide swath of educational, socioeconomic and other well-worn marketing categories; conventional marketing demographics tools can't pin them down. Perhaps that's because *understanding values* is more critical for businesses that want to court a successful relationship with this breed. These consumers make purchases using fundamentally different criteria not based solely on a product's features and benefits, but also on how the product contributes to their health, plus the health of others and the planet. Frequently, these consumers even forego convenience to find products and services that align with their conscience.

From flavors of ice cream (plain old vanilla to Ben & Jerry's *One Sweet Whirled*) to the plethora of spiritual books (over 37,000 titles on Amazon.com alone and growing[9]) to automobiles of every color (basic black to Jaguar's Aspen Green), every consumer today is bombarded with an unrivaled amount of options. In the U.S. alone, close to 32,000 new products were announced in 2002, up from the few thousand introduced in 1970.[10] How does this breed respond? With their heads, their hearts and their wallets combined. Using their values as a filter to steer through the maze of alternatives, this breed makes sophisticated choices about the brands they purchase with their health, the larger environment and the future in mind.

Words like *experience, wellness, authenticity, learning, fulfillment, relationship* and *personal power* uniquely speak to this breed.[11] These aren't just words; this breed of consumer uses these words to architect life on their own terms. Rather than merely react to appeals by the latest marketing scheme, this consumer pursues brands which help create a lifestyle that's personally and socially relevant, easier and centered in the heart of their values.

These consumers wield significant and growing social power. They are more than just a market niche; they are the *opinion leaders that sway the decisions* of an additional 39 percent of the population leaning toward lifestyles of health and sustainability, another 83 million consumers.[12] Since this breed spends an estimated $230 billion in U.S. sales and represents untapped possibilities worldwide,[13] companies right and left are scurrying to capture their attention.

It's no revelation that these consumers are enticed by products and

Consumers are frequently investing with their spiritual and social values. Business issues often driving their investments are "corporate ethics, followed by product safety, involvement in sweatshops, environmental impact, labor relations, and equal employment opportunity." [14]

organizations that not only sell them a means to health and well-being, but set an example of it as well. In fact, 90 percent of consumers in this breed say they buy products from companies whose values for health and sustainability are aligned with their own.[15] This breed is literally using life-centric values to navigate a complex, and, oftentimes, confusing marketplace.

Two defining characteristics of consumers who want lifestyles of health and sustainability are: 1) they are willing to pay up to 20 percent more for products and services that generate personal and societal wellness, and 2) they naturally teach family and friends about the benefits of the products and services they choose, becoming a viable marketing avenue to boost company sales. Now, that's something to pay attention to![16]

A New Breed of Worker

Consumers aren't the only ones using new values to redesign their choices. An emerging breed of worker is reshaping the nature of work and workplaces, and, as a result, your organization's capabilities. Take, for instance, Marie, a free-lance writer for a host of business magazines.

Marie started her career in her early twenties as an editor for a large publishing house. Enthusiastic about her work, she exceeded every challenge she was given. Her passion clearly showed in results. The books she fashioned were top-notch and sought after. To reward her for so many jobs well done, Marie was upgraded to a management role. Quite an achievement for a woman of her young age! Yet, after only a few years, she found that she no longer enjoyed going to work. The luster of her new role wore thin, and she missed using the writing skills she could remember loving since she was a little girl. So, she quit her job and set up her own shop as a free-lance writer for business publications. The security of a paycheck wasn't enough to keep her tied to an organization where she couldn't find a clear-cut creative outlet. A gain for Marie, yet a considerable loss of creative competence for her former company.

Whether dubbed *free agents*[17] or the *creative class*[18], a new breed of worker is more motivated to use their creative intelligence than to make money. Yes, money is essential to their lives, but something else attracts them. The *way* they work and *what* they produce is as significant to them as the paycheck, bonuses and office perks. They aren't interested in work draining the life out of them. And, they aren't inspired by routine McJobs.[19]

> "It isn't enough that we have 'meaningful' work. What is also required is work that satisfies the soul." [20]
>
> Thomas Moore, former Catholic monk and author

This kind of employee doesn't swallow the line that professional success comes from moving up the ladder or necessarily being loyal to one company. As layoffs became an accepted business strategy over the past decade, any allegiance these employees had to one corporation faded into the sunset. These workers now trade in seemingly secure jobs for work opportunities that align with their basic identity as *creators*. They concentrate in environments (cities, social communities, workplaces and the like) that stimulate their ingenuity, and they launch businesses to work for themselves. Plus, they use new forms of self-management (such as flexible schedules and horizontal promotions) when working for others and experiment with novel employer/employee arrangements as ad hoc contractors.

Free agents are estimated at 33 million strong in the U.S., larger than the manufacturing and government workforce combined.[21] The creative class is guessed to be 38 million, with creative professionals of every age and ethnicity spanning all industries.[22] By either count, this breed is over one third of the nation's workforce, a force you must reckon with. Whether they are inside or outside conventional organizations, these workers apply the values they identify with most: creative expression, independent judgment, diversity, openness, experimentation, individuality and meaningful employment. With these values as their guide, they generate novel ways to bring their spirit and intellect fully to work, and they re-examine the role work plays in defining personal success.

> "When enough people demand that work be nourishing and fulfilling, companies will find they have to make it so in order to attract and hold the most creative people." [23]
>
> Willis Harman, author and Co-Founder, World Business Academy

At the top of their game, women leaders are willing to make gutsy decisions to opt out of traditional career tracks in order to experience a worklife that aligns with their values. "... a recent survey by the research firm Catalyst found that 26 percent of women at the cusp of the most senior levels of management don't want the promotion. ...*Fortune* magazine found that of the 108 women who have appeared on its list of the top 50 most powerful women over the years, at least 20 have chosen to leave their high-powered jobs, most voluntarily, for lives that are less intense and more fulfilling." [24]

Whether as employee or contractor, this breed of worker is likely part of your workforce. Yet, reacting to them isn't about catering to whims for flex-time. This growing breed represents a much bigger issue. These workers are becoming a powerful social class, mushrooming in size, with even broader implications for business.

Creative capital theory, a new wave in economics, talks about these implications well: this breed of worker possesses the main resource—*creativity*—that generates growth for organizations and geographies alike.[25] While information and technology drove progress in the past, progress today is powered by ingenious people, your *creative capital*. Just as you'd manage financial capital, utilizing creative capital wisely enhances your organization's ability to innovate, generate jobs and grow financially.[26]

Today's markets demand that organizations uncompromisingly generate and apply new ideas to even survive. Sustained innovation is the name of the game. As a consequence, this new breed of worker is indispensable. They are the labor pool's creative know-how. You must appeal to their values to attract and retain them as creative talent, and you must maximize their imagination to radically improve your organization's performance.

"...economic growth is powered by creative people, who prefer places that are diverse, tolerant and open to new ideas. Diversity increases the odds that a place will attract different

types of creative people with different skill sets and ideas. Places with diverse mixes of creative people are more likely to generate new combinations. Furthermore, diversity and concentration work together to speed the flow of knowledge. Greater and more diverse concentrations of creative capital in turn lead to higher rates of innovation, high-technology business formation, job generation and economic growth." [27]

A New Breed of Business

A new breed of business is also on the rise. These businesses strive to bridge the wide gulf between their company goals and their business realities. Yet for these companies, this gap is a chance to advance health-seeking innovations and projects, not a problem to be solved.

Realizing that the world's natural resources can't continue to meet modern demands, Hewlett-Packard's (HP) CEO Carly Fiorina and her predecessors are leading the company to find ways to prevent the pollution of manufacturing computer hardware and minimize the impact of the company's products on the environment. Alone, their eco-friendly approaches are nothing new. In fact, eco-friendliness is the market's baseline expectations of business. But, the company is taking an additional step. HP is re-envisioning a world that's completely networked, where natural resources aren't overtaxed and where there is "less stuff and more value." [28] It is inventing totally new solutions that reframe the environmental challenge to one of opportunity. With this impetus, a core business strategy of HP is to sell more e-services to limit hardware production and, consequently, lessen demands on the environment. HP is striving to turn a controversial issue, such as the use of natural resources, into business and social innovation.

Social and environmental challenges force progressive business to reflect on the effects of its values, motivations and actions. For instance, as companies have married the urge for immediate profit with the drive to produce pioneering

technology, the reach of computers has dramatically grown while the shelf life has radically dropped. Today, more than 50% of U.S. households own a computer, upgrading to new computers every two years, a terrific trend for companies who profit from computer sales. Yet, what about the rising numbers of computers to be discarded? In 1997, the U.S. Environmental Protection Agency claimed that over 3.2 million tons of e-waste already packed landfills, a number estimated at fourfold that amount by 2003. By 2005, they forecast that "one computer will become obsolete for every new computer on the market," creating an escalating e-waste pileup with significant polluting effects.[29] What responsibility does the computer industry have to balance the push for faster computing against the toxic effects to natural and human life?

The Dow Jones Group Sustainability Index (DJGSI) reflects companies dedicated to corporate citizenship and social responsibility. Studied over a 5-year period, DJGSI companies performed on average 36.1 percent better than did regular Dow Jones companies. "Companies that take a strategic approach to corporate citizenship are likely to be well managed overall."[32]

Driven by legal requirements, social demands or plain common sense, like Hewlett-Packard, the new breed of business knows that healthy financial returns rely on a healthy society. Companies in this breed have learned that managing business to quarterly profit goals clashes with the basic purpose they seek to deliver: *to be a sound, profitable engine of growth and contribution that stakeholders can trust for the long haul.* These companies are citizens of the world, interested in more than just their corner of the market.

Contemporary companies must keep up with the aspirations of societies worldwide, such as peace, ecological stability, workplace safety, free trade and human rights.[30] This isn't about corporate goodwill; it is about business staying in rhythm with what matters to stakeholders. Corporate responsibility is "an increasingly important variable in the traditional profit-loss calculation"[31] that this new breed of business uses to measure success. These companies experience the same challenges as every other company, but they respond by breaking new ground for better ways to generate sustained financial and social value. They continually show the rest of the corporate world how it can be done.

These businesses are accountable, truthful and transparent in their approaches, and they operate with a clear set of values for health and sustainability inspired from their core. They don't compromise conscientious business practices. Instead, they build business systems through enlightened governance, and they hold an intentional business strategy to behave on the up and up. They know that this is the only viable route to foster a superior reputation, supply the highest quality of products and services, market to sophisticated consumers, manage their risks, recruit the best people and maintain financial resilience even in times of market unrest.

> **A recent poll found that only 23 percent of Americans believed "the bosses of large corporations could be trusted." Ironically, 50 percent of the company's profitability and reputation can be attributed to the individual effect of its CEO.[34] A European survey further found that 'loss of reputation' is the second biggest threat to competitiveness.[35]**

> **In 2001, 50 percent of the world's largest companies produced environmental, social and corporate citizenship reports alongside or integrated within their yearly financial reports, the highest percentage ever.[33]**

Challenges and Opportunities the New Breeds Hold for Your Leadership

The emerging life-centric value system reflects a mounting demand in society and the marketplace for greater health, accountability, creative expression and sustainability. This value system shows up in at least three avenues vital to business: a new profile of sophisticated consumers who sway market decisions, highly creative workers who are more loyal to using their creativity than to any particular company, and businesses that employ progressive and responsible methods for success. Each of these three new breeds is questioning conventional rules and authority about how to live, work and achieve results.

Why should you care? Because, whether you know it or not, the combined power of these three breeds *already* challenge your company's ability to deliver and sustain results. Today, a growing population of consumers, workers and businesses actively use their values for quality of life, health and sustainability in order to make decisions, and they can be a key or an obstacle to your success. Thus, these three breeds present you with both business challenges and opportunities.

Challenges ● ● ● ● ● ● ● ● ● ● Opportunities

Conscientious Consumers

Consumers who hold companies to a higher standard than simply providing a breadth of low priced and convenient goods and services. Now, what you stand for as a company and how your products contribute to society impacts your profitability.

Billion Dollar Market

A $230 billion and growing market of consumers who are:
• intensely brand-loyal
• highly influential over family and friends
• swaying a shift toward healthier choices worldwide
• less sensitive to the price of products and services.

Wary Investors

Investors who (thanks to the Internet and media) can and do scrutinize the details of corporate governance. And, they will rapidly punish your stock at the slightest sign of impropriety.

A Reputation of Integrity

A chance to create a company brand that radiates integrity—one that contributes to a greater good, is resilient in economic downturns and stands on its own ethics before the scrutiny of consumers, workers and investors alike.

Enlightened Workers

Workers who are more apt to define the terms of their work with or without a company. Other priorities (health, family, where they live, personal dreams and so on) now take precedence.

Creative Capital

A pool of professionals whose values, work and life styles highly correlate with the fundamental driver of our economy: *creativity*, the critical resource for all new technologies, knowledge, industries and sustainable wealth.

Ethics Requirements

Governments, social action groups, non-governmental organizations, vendors and customers who require—whether through legal means or social pressures—a higher standard of ethics and accountability before entertaining the idea of doing business with you.

Better Partnerships

Stronger business partnerships based on mutual advantage, values, trust and accountability. These healthier relationships enable shared innovations and business practices to emerge, such as radical product designs and cross-marketing. All parties capitalize on these win-win approaches.

Short-Sighted Leaders

Leaders who rely on traditional, ineffective and even harmful modes of decision-making, based on business models designed to manage the company purely to a short-term financial bottom line.

Progressive Leadership

Leaders who understand how to:
• manage and measure performance based on a broader definition of business success
• work with complex systems
• choose the most powerful actions for healthy financial and societal returns.

Consider it this way. The emerging life-centric values add to the inescapable turbulence companies already encounter in today's business climate. Through the new breeds of consumer, worker and business, these values are intensifying a sense of crises that is demanding change. Like with every crisis, companies can choose from a continuum of responses:

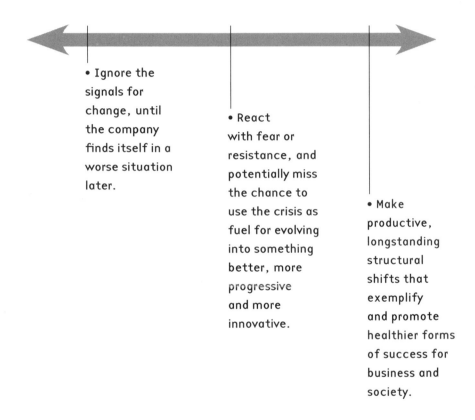

• Ignore the signals for change, until the company finds itself in a worse situation later.

• React with fear or resistance, and potentially miss the chance to use the crisis as fuel for evolving into something better, more progressive and more innovative.

• Make productive, longstanding structural shifts that exemplify and promote healthier forms of success for business and society.

21st Century Leadership in Action:

Addressing Challenges and Opportunities

Reflect on the list of Challenges and Opportunities in the table on page 37. Ask the following questions with a group of leaders in your organization:

☑ *How do these Challenges and Opportunities relate to our business success today and in the future?*

☑ *Where are we already seeing these Challenges in our business environment? How are we responding? Is our response effective? If not, what might we do to respond with a wider vision, effectiveness, innovation and accountability?*

☑ *Are we capitalizing on these Opportunities? If not, why not? Where have we 'missed the boat?' If we are taking advantage of these Opportunities, how are our approaches delivering value for us and for others?*

☑ *What do these Challenges and Opportunities mean for the type of leadership we need to cultivate in our business?*

The 21st Century Leader:
Driven by Wellth

The new breeds of consumer, worker and business provide plenty of challenges and opportunities to make any good leader take notice. Yet, for progressive 21st century leaders, these breeds reflect a deeper tide of change: all of humankind is being stretched to learn how to operate from values which create total health and effectiveness on a widespread scale. Regardless of title, role, color or gender, the disruptions in our world environment are demanding all of us to "shift our perspectives, deepen our perception, often against a great deal of resistance, [and] to embrace the deeper and wider context."[36] For people courageous enough to step into leadership both as a public role and a stance to life, the emerging life-centric values are evolving conventional management thinking into a more enlightened 21st century leadership mind.

This is a tall order, but 21st century leaders are the only ones who can make positive change happen.

And, 21st century leaders must be the nexus of positive change. No other living system that we know of has the extent that humans do to intentionally direct thoughts and behaviors toward preferred outcomes. Whether regarded as spiritual or biological beings, humans are inherently creators. The act of creating is an essential part of our nature. As 21st century leaders, one of our imperatives is to turn that creative intelligence into meaningful value and results.

All of humankind is being stretched to learn how to operate from values which create total health and effectiveness on a widespread scale.

Humans conceptualize and connect ideas, often inventing something original in the process. They produce mental and physical tools of every sort to suit their purposes. They can forecast potential consequences of their actions and make decisions today with tomorrow in mind. They organize ethnic groups, professional societies and whole cultures around value systems that give them a sense of significance. And, humans can learn from their mistakes and reflect on their place in the larger scheme of things. The human capacity to create and to learn from what's created is endless. However, it must be harnessed in healthier ways to meet the needs of contemporary life.

Ironically, for all the creative talent humans possess, no other living system has been as damaging to life as people have. Human consciousness is a powerful tool to create, yet *what* humans create is too often destructive.

Driven by their deepest values to enhance and evolve life, 21st century leaders strive to channel the creative power of entire human systems into relevant, generative and sustainable outcomes. They start by asking a simple question.

What are we creating for?

21st century leaders want to know of their businesses: What is the drive behind the results we create and the business strategies we choose?

Are we seeking to gain …

- Power?

- Loyalty?

- Money and material wealth?

- Harmony with the natural and social world?

- Outcomes that transcend all of these?

If a function of commercial enterprise is to generate profit, our profit is *for the sake of what*? Given the complexities already evident in the 21st century, profit clearly isn't a reliable end game by itself. What else, beyond profit, do we generate? Is our company producing something that we deem 'good' purely because people buy it, or does what we produce contribute to healthier, more sustainable benefits? Do we even know how to create something that's profitable *and* healthy *and* sustainable?

What are we creating for? This is an enormous question, one that 21st century leaders use to navigate complexities and orient their leadership. Why? Because these leaders aren't interested in perpetuating ideas, behaviors, policies and institutions that produce ill effects. They seek to turn systems of disease and exhaustion into solutions for health and effectiveness. To disrupt the corporate circuitry of fear-based actions in order to drive toward the generation of enlightened results. 21st century leaders focus on how they and their organizations can productively channel creative power, and they are set apart from others by an unshakable urge to benefit people, nature, commerce and society. The health and evolution of life is the first and foremost reason 21st century leaders create anything at all.

"What's your obligation to keep the future alive?"[37]

C.K. Pralahad, President & CEO, Praja Inc.

This isn't a purely altruistic act or a public relations ploy as some people might think. Authentic 21st century leaders believe that finding broader and more progressive measures of success from which to create is the only clear strategy for healthy, sustainable performance for business and the larger world.

Instead of treating new markets, breakthrough technologies and business profits as savior, 21st century leaders see these as instruments of positive, long-lasting change. Instead of expanding their organizations and their brands for the sake of reputation or size, they use the creative power of their organizations and brands for the sake of greater well-being no matter where they are. These leaders work with the intrinsic human drive to create, instead of working against it, in order to generate progressive forms of success. This is simply the worldview from which they lead.

> **Authentic 21st century leaders believe that finding broader and more progressive measures of success from which to create is the only clear strategy for healthy, sustainable performance in business and the larger world.**

In organizations and endeavors of all types, 21st century leaders are attempting to construct trustworthy engines of success out of inspired purposes and enduring principles. They strive to transform the traditional economic tenet 'grow or die' to a more enlightened 21st century principle: *grow mindfully and thrive.*[38]

It may seem like it takes the resources of a huge company to be healthy, profitable, contributing and sustainable. But, nothing could be farther from the truth. Beginning as quite a small organization, two partners from Michigan are already taking the road less traveled to success. When in 1982 Ari Weinzweig and Paul Saginaw opened Zingerman's Deli in Ann Arbor, they were frustrated by the "conventional business model that saw the employees as disposable and food as overhead." They wanted to give customers a fabulous product, provide employees a respectful and caring work environment, promote the worldwide Slow Food movement so that small-demand and rare foods didn't disappear, and contribute to the vitality of their local community.

They've obviously found a recipe that works! Since their inception, Zingerman's has drawn from home-grown talent and

ingredients wherever feasible to expand beyond the small deli business in a way that also stimulates the local economy. They now operate a creamery, a mail-order company, a bakehouse, a catering operation and an Americana-themed restaurant, which produced $20.7 million combined in 2003 by July. They also manage Food Gatherers, a service that distributes millions of pound of food to those in need every year.

As a core business approach, these leaders have learned to allow about two years to fully incubate each expansion of Zingerman's using the system of vendors, employees and members of the community for support. This lets them launch new enterprises mindfully given their higher aspirations and their values for health and sustainability.

For Weinzweig and Saginaw, sustained business growth occurs through passion, purpose, a sense of community and principled, well-managed strategies that account for compelling social and business benefits. "Growing this way attracts great people. If it went faster, we'd lose who we are," says Weinzberg.[39]

21st century leaders bring healthy results, healthy people and a healthy world together. They've braved the old assumptions about competition and growth, and now seek to contribute to a shift in worldwide values where purposeful creation, health and sustainability are integral. Through inspired enterprises, they expect to foster organizations and a world that are decent, alive and compassionate.

This leader doesn't consider business as separate from life. Perhaps this sentiment is said best by Sufi teacher, Hazrat Inayat Khan:

"…the purpose of life is to arrive at that stage where every moment becomes fruitful. And what does fruitful mean? Does it mean fruits for oneself? No, trees do not bear fruit for themselves, but for others. True profit is not that profit which one makes for oneself, true profit is that which one makes for others. After attaining all that one wants to attain, be it earthly or heavenly, what is the results of it all? The result is only this, that all that one has attained, that one has acquired, whether earthly or heavenly, one can place before others."[40]

Essentially, the 21st century leader is using the pains and possibilities of civilization to carve out a whole new consciousness for living, working and leading. They are bringing greater mindfulness to their decisions, noticing how they too play small or divisively at times, and they stretch themselves to generate grander, more beneficial effects. When they put life-centric values into action, the genuine consequence is *wellth*: an integral result that redefines the traditional notion of wealth. Wellth uniquely produces greater health and effectiveness by uniting the drives for economic, human and ecological value.

Chapter 3 talks more about 'wellth,' the 21st century leaders' mantra.

Chapter Highlights

- *A new set of life-centric values is emerging in society, and it is inspiring change in three spheres intimately tied to your company's success: a new breed of consumers, a new breed of workers and a new breed of business.*

- *The new breed of consumer is an estimated 30 percent of our population who are motivated by issues of health and sustainability in business and society.*

- *The new breed of worker is the free agent employee, contractor and vendor who determines success on his own terms rather than on the goalposts set by organizations.*

- *The new breed of business is a growing fraternity of companies which realize that paving the way for a successful future relies on a healthy society.*

- *The 21st century leader knows that the new breeds of consumer, worker and business are more than challenges and opportunities; these breeds reflect a deeper current of change. All of humankind is being stretched to learn how to operate from values which create total health and effectiveness on a widespread scale.*

- *So the 21st century leader asks of themselves and their organizations: What are we creating for?*

wellth

"It is no longer sufficient to be a smart organization, one that can scan the commercial environment, detect variations, and react accordingly... Our business organizations need to become conscious of the evolutionary role business plays in the future of the planet and to take responsibility for that role. ... in the 21st century, companies that learn from and imitate nature in order to operate in harmony with natural laws will be more successful and profitable than those that don't. The evolutionary corporation operates with a wider vision of its purpose, an expanded definition of its business environment, and a sense of evolutionary responsibility. This task is both daunting and enormously exciting. It engages the very best in human ingenuity while it invites us to be humble in view of the immensity of what we still do not know."[1]

Brian Nattrass and Mary Altomare, sustainability professionals

---

"When the goal of economic activity is seen to be satisfaction of desires, economic activity is open-ended and without clear definition—desires are endless. ...economic activity must be controlled by the qualification that it is directed to the attainment of well-being rather than the 'maximum satisfaction' sought after by traditional economic thinking. Well-being as an objective acts as a control on economic activity. No longer are we struggling against each other to satisfy endless desires. Instead, our activities are directed toward the attainment of well-being. If economic activity is directed in this way, its objectives are clear and its activities are controlled. A balance or equilibrium is achieved. There is no excess, no overconsumption, no overproduction."[2]

Venerable P.A. Payutto, Buddhist scholar

wellth

the 21st century leader's central drive

Wellth **is the progressive** 21st century leadership drive to achieve and, more importantly, sustain results in the healthiest way possible. It's the integrated financial, human and ecological gains that answer the 21st century leaders' defining question: *What are we creating for?* Wellth signifies the values of health and effectiveness that 21st century leaders use to moderate their pursuits.

In today's environment, wellth is the 21st century leader's edge, how these leaders distinctively put creative intelligence into real-time action. As a cornerstone of the contemporary redefinition of the world, wellth is the new vanguard of consumers, workers and businesses from all walks of life who are crafting an authentic, life-centric existence.

Wellth is a fundamentally new way of seeing our circumstances. It's an appreciation that our lives and our businesses don't have to be run as a zero-sum game where there are only winners and losers. Incorporating the ideas and strategies for generating wellth into everyday business activity is the 21st century leader's core task.

Wellth is about the company you keep. It is the generation of sustainable value that's felt by society as much as it is the companies that produce it.

You may have already noticed that wellth is a play on the word *wealth*, commonly defined as "goods and resources having economic value."[3] Interestingly enough, the word wealth comes from the Middle English root, wela, meaning "good health," a root that is also the core of "well" and "wellness." Wellth combines these two ideas—sound economics and good health—to create a more integral aspiration: *the generation of sustainable value that's felt by society as much as it is the companies that produce it.*

The Wellth-Driven Company

Wellth is about the company you keep. It re-shapes everything concerning your business, from the way your organization reacts to marketplace and social developments to the way you treat your creative capital to the way your business model operates altogether.

> "When asked what challenges his company faces in balancing financial interests with social obligations, Bruce Anderson, CEO of Wilson TurboPower Inc. is quick to answer: Huh? It's not that Anderson doesn't understand the question. It's just that his business sees a wide-open market opportunity, making a question about trade-offs largely unanswerable. No zero-sum game here. It turns out that profit and social responsibility are mutually inclusive after all."
>
> "The company's first product, the regenerator, works with microturbines, units that resemble backup generators, except that they provide a source of primary, not secondary, power for a limited area like a small group of office buildings, alleviating many of the headaches associated with centralized utility grids. The Wilson TurboPower regenerator takes waste heat from microturbines and puts it to other uses, such as heating water, boosting efficiency from about 30% to 80%."
>
> "The fact that Wilson TurboPower faces essentially no trade-off between its bottom line and its benefit to society hits upon a fundamental point about corporate responsibility: It doesn't have to be an either-or choice, like picking decaf over regular. And it's not just about philanthropy ..."[4]

☉ Wellth generates progressive business results.

21st century leaders and their companies strive to steward wellth-driven organizations, inspired by the wide-ranging social and business results this conscientious and creative approach can bring. Wellth-seeking companies often find rewards in one or more of eight areas:

• New contracts and contract renewals
• Generative, loyal client relationships

• Streamlined and eco-friendly procurement practices, workplaces and operations

• Business, government, non-governmental and community alliances based on values for mutual success

• Resilience in times of major change and crisis
• A legacy that makes a long-lasting impression

• A knack for innovating and learning
• The ability to transform social ills into social and business benefit
• Effective decisions between people and functions without the need for tight controls

• Greater financial returns
• Higher stock valuation
• Access to capital and investments in markets that were once off limits

• A corporate and brand reputation and image that appeals to the growing population of healthy consumers
• Forays into untapped wellth-driven markets

• Invigorated employees
• Retention of talented people
• Lower absenteeism, turnover and healthcare costs
• A culture of wellth that attracts the creative capital required for sustained innovation

But the positive impact of wellth-driven activities doesn't stop with the organization. These activities often establish healthier standards for an entire marketplace. For example, when the U.S. government decided to purchase only energy-efficient computer equipment in 1993, it "set in motion a massive overhaul of the consumer market." As a result, 95 percent of monitors, 80 percent of computers, and 99 percent of printers sold in North America today meet Energy Star ratings.[5]

➁ Wellth redefines business' measures of success.

Wellth is a new driver for 21st century business, not just the ambition of so called 'green' companies. It's simply a better, futuristic and more balanced approach for commercial success. Wellth simultaneously attends to the goals of business for longevity, societies' aspirations for a healthier world and the natural principles for creating sustainable results. (Chapter 5 teaches you these principles through our framework, *The 7 Essentials*[sm].) Wellth-driven leaders know that issues related to ecology, human rights and community development are no longer peripheral to business; today they are the central limiting or accelerating factors to business growth.[7]

> "The biggest impetus for change in business practices is not a growing sense of social responsibility, but market forces—concerned customers, vocal employees, and pragmatic investors who are worried about the value of their holdings. What was once regarded as nice-to-do has become have-to-do."[6]
>
> David Grayson, Director, Business in the Community, and Adrian Hodges, Managing Director, The Prince of Wales International Business Leaders Forum

Consider a story from The Coca-Cola Company that plays out in many global corporations. Through an unparalleled distribution system and a trusted brand, consumers in nearly 200 countries enjoy Coca-Cola products at a rate of more than a billion servings a day. From drink to drink, the company strives to deliver the core promise that inspired it from day one: to refresh and benefit everyone it touches. Yet, company leaders realize an extra dimension colors 21st century organizations. Leaders aspire to use methods that sustain the health of their business as well as the societies in which they operate. In developing markets, for instance, the company initiates thousands of micro-businesses, from financing upstart kiosks in South Africa to donating mobile pushcarts to disadvantaged women in Vietnam. These micro-businesses are a win-win proposition: they sell Coca-Cola products and other sundries, stimulate local economies, encourage the entrepreneurial spirit of individuals, create new jobs and build sustainable livelihoods for impoverished families.[8] For developing societies and global companies like Coca-Cola, well-managed micro-businesses can generate a revolving cycle of wellth.

Wellth expands our ideas about success well beyond profit. Of course making a profit is fundamental to the survival and growth of every commercial organization. But, it isn't sufficient for the organization's long-term performance. Management scholar Charles Hampden Turner suggests a few reasons why:[9]

> **"Profit comes too late to steer by."** Profit is a measure of success based on the interplay of ideas and actions implemented by the company long ago. As a result, by the time profit appears, the realities of the business have already considerably changed. Although profit is one useful gauge of the past, it is an undependable beacon with which to navigate the company into the unknowns of the future.

> **"Profit conflicts with values of equal importance yet higher priority."** By giving profit a special status above all else, leaders can make decisions that erode the organization's long-term profitability. For the company's lasting health, of equal or higher priority are values like upgrading the company's competitive capabilities, protecting its reputation and brands, managing its internal operations with integrity and making a positive difference in the societies in which it conducts business. Ironically, what leaders usually want for their companies is *healthy, sustained growth*, yet they mistakenly use profit as the only growth indicator. Driven by a narrow and pressurized spotlight on profit, leaders get into the bad habit of attending to human and global issues as a sideline or missing these essential issues altogether. Time and time again, companies find this a recipe for courting disaster.

"The past decade may well be remembered as the era of the bold, high-flying, 'sky's the limit' leader. ...corner-office titans graced the covers of business magazines, and the public seemed fascinated with their willingness to flaunt the rules and break from the corporate herd with incredible daring and flair. But like Icarus, they flew too high. Scandal set in, and these once feted and envied leaders found themselves falling hard and fast." These leaders "suffer from 'winner-wants-all' mindset. ... just when they appear to have it all, these A-list performers demonstrate uncharacteristic lapses in professional judgment or personal conduct." They "develop a dangerous aversion to moderation."[10]

"When imitated by factions or persons within the corporation, profit orientation becomes suboptimal." Maximizing company profit as the sole reason for operating is, by design, a self-centric motive. Companies directed in this way should expect the same self-centric motivations from every department, team and worker. Paradoxically, most leaders want people in their organizations to exercise radical innovation, collaboration, well-managed action and learning, all skills necessary for sustained competitiveness in a global and complex environment. But, the profit motive doesn't emphasize these skills; in fact, it teaches quite the reverse.

"Profitability is an organic not a mechanical attribute." Profitability provides the means to innovations and wide-reaching impact; it isn't a solitary definition of success or an endpoint all by itself. Creating a business engine for sustained profitability parallels the rhythm of an evolving living system; it is organic, with cycles of peaks, valleys and plateaus. In this cycle, profitability *emerges* because of the interactions between stakeholders, such as companies, colleges, social alliances, workers, communities and governments. When these relationships are healthy, they weather instability, innovate and learn. And, they are more likely to generate profitability for the business system over the long haul.

It's clear that wellth includes the profit motive, yet uses that motive for purposes of serving a higher-reaching drive: *the healthy advancement of the company combined with the evolution of life.*

⊚ Wellth grows the company's "credibility capital."

Wellth-driven companies build what sociologist Paul Ray calls credibility capital,[12] a resilient relationship with the public that's an invaluable business asset. This kind of capital is fostered when companies walk their talk, putting their values for health and sustainability into reliable actions, excellent products and services, and responsible, well-managed results. Ray even suggests that, like a capital stock, credibility capital can accumulate; a company's actions buoy it or destroy it over time.

Credibility capital profits a company in good times and bad. In good times, it reinforces a loyal public following; in bad times, partners, consumers, investors and citizens are more apt to trust what the company says, give the company the benefit of the doubt and restrain from actions (such as lawsuits) that could considerably hurt the company's reputation and performance.[13]

The desire to build credibility capital with wellth-driven consumers can even make for strange corporate bedfellows, like those emerging in the food and beverage industry. Through acquisition, investment and partnerships, multinational giants such as Dean Foods, Kraft, General Mills, Coca-Cola and McDonalds have joined with smaller organics firms like Horizon, Boca Burger, Cascadian Farms, Odwalla and Newman's Own. While the longer-term results of these marriages are unknown, the short-term effects are evident. Organics are opening multinationals to profitable health-conscious markets, while multinationals are globalizing the values of health and sustainability through the pervasive sales and distribution of organic products.[15] Utilizing strategies to cultivate credibility capital, like the partnerships between multinationals and organics, is one way that wellth-driven companies connect with consumers, manage their risks and generate business alliances from an undeniable wellth-centered core.

☻ Wellth inspires the 21st century leader's legacy.

Not an ego-based legacy, but a creative, life-enhancing contribution to the ongoing evolution of the whole. 21st century leaders aren't driven solely by what they can get. They are just as driven by what they can give back. They know that shifting our financial, human and ecological burdens to future generations doesn't bode well for civilization or ongoing business success. Consequently, the legacy of 21st century leaders is both the privilege and the responsibility to develop the next age of leaders and initiatives that foster the values of health and sustainability around the globe. These leaders create opportunities to cultivate wellth-driven leadership today to set the stage for a healthier tomorrow.

"...21st-century new-paradigm thinkers are easily recognized. Status, the revenge motive, feelings of guilt or shame, or the preoccupation with power are simply not valued."[16]

Warren Bennis, Jagdish Parikh & Ronnie Essem, *Beyond Leadership: Balancing Economics, Ethics and Ecology*

☻ Wellth guides enlightened leadership decisions.

Progressive 21st century companies are guided by the idea that aspirations of wellth aren't elusive. These far-reaching ambitions are possible. So, these companies relentlessly ask the tougher questions that other companies shy away from, such as:

- *How will we allow measures of wellth, rather than narrow measures of profitability, to drive our company?*

- *How will wellth-driven measures shape our decisions, actions and leadership?*

- *What ground-breaking business and economic models will we use to promote a healthier 21st century for our company and the world?*

- *What products and services will we consciously offer to advance the wellth of our consumers and our partners?*

- *How will we contribute to a culture of wellth, inside and outside our company, no matter where we operate?*

Swedish-born IKEA is a good example of an organization that doesn't shy away from wellth-conscious decisions. Today, the company is the only furniture retailer in the U.S. that maintains PBDE-free products. PBDE (polybrominated diphenyl ether), a flame retardant utilized in foam cushions, is considered "one of the most dangerous chemicals in common use today."[17] Yet, even with the growing health risks PBDE causes people and wildlife, it is still a $30-million-a-year market. IKEA's decision to use safer flame retardants was remarkable; it *raised* the cost of IKEA's U.S. furniture by 10 percent, a sizeable amount in a cutthroat industry. Magnus Bjork, senior compliance manager at IKEA North America says that the decision "pays off in the long run. What costs you have, you can gain back with consumer confidence."[18]

Wellth reflects a powerful new thought for 21st century leaders who are shifting to progressive models of business and social excellence. Simply put, the philosophy of wellth signifies a different way of leading business altogether.

21st Century Leadership in Action:
Aligning Our Business toward Wellth

Think about the definition of wellth you've learned in this chapter. Ask the following questions of yourself or a group of leaders in your organization:

☑ *How will we allow measures of wellth, rather than narrow measures of profitability, to drive our company?*

☑ *How will wellth-driven measures shape our decisions, actions and leadership?*

☑ *What ground-breaking business and economic models could we use to promote a healthier 21st century for our company and the world?*

☑ *What products and services could we consciously offer to advance the wellth of our consumers and our partners?*

☑ *How will we contribute to a culture of wellth, inside and outside our company, no matter where we operate?*

The Wellth-Driven Life

Make no mistake. The notion of wellth doesn't just apply to business. It applies to you personally.

Among other things, a wellth-driven life is an active integration of a sound mind, a fit body, a sense of belonging and purpose, and a healthy range of emotional expression. In fact, one Stanford study of 53 *naturally successful* leaders, including physicians, authors, philanthropists, managers and others, found that these leaders not only take care of their whole health, they also draw on it as a resource to meet their challenges, solve complex problems, innovate and effectively lead.[19] Wellth, then, isn't merely the outcome of how you live and lead; it is a resource for living and leading itself.

> The most successful leaders not only take care of their whole health, they also draw on it as a resource to meet their challenges, solve complex problems, innovate and effectively lead.

On the contrary, the lack of wellth can erode your leadership. Take for instance the dilemma of some CEOs who spend their entire careers focused on their organizations' performance, yet find their individual health deteriorates as a result. A 1999 report from the World Economic Forum shows that, ironically, the personal well-being of CEOs directly affects the health of their business. "CEOs are increasingly suffering from stress, sleep deprivation, heart disease, loneliness, failed marriages, and depression, among other problems. And those woes are taking toll on the bottom-line."[20] Unhealthy CEOs, as well as leaders at all levels, lack the stamina, clear-headedness, emotional grit and world-centric awareness to make the best decisions for the organization as a whole. Without good health and well-being, these leaders are unable to access the depth of awareness and wisdom that could help them lead their lives, their projects and their businesses altogether better.

On the following pages is the *"Personal Wellth Quotient,"* a checklist that outlines a few of the qualities and behaviors wellth-driven leaders capitalize on. Assess your wellth quotient to determine how you can take advantage of your whole health in order to enhance your leadership performance.

Personal Wellth Quotient

Instructions: Rate yourself on each of the thirty questions below using a scale of 1 to 5. A rating of 1 means "This is *never* true for me," and 5 means "This is *always* true for me." Put your answers in the space provided, and tally your final score.

Never true   Always true

1   **2**   **3**   **4**   **5**

____I regularly engage in some form of physical activity (three to five times per week).

____I get enough sleep and relaxation to recharge my body and mind.

____I regularly engage in some form of spiritual practice (such as prayer, reflective journaling, meditation or mindfulness training, worship with a spiritual community and so on).

____I am mentally stimulated by my life and work.

____I use external substances (such as drugs, alcohol, natural remedies, caffeine and so on) only as appropriate. I do not over-depend on these substances for things I can learn to do without them.

____I regularly practice some form of self-care and play (such as massage, hobbies and so on).

____I can experience and express a full range of emotions. The emotions I express are appropriate to the situation at hand.

____I use stressors (such as anxiety, fatigue, physical ailments, broken relationships and crises) as signals for making healthier choices about my life and work. I know what a healthy amount of stress is for me.

___I trust that all situations in life are fluid and open to new possibility. Consequently, I embrace new ideas and change.

___I live and work in physical surroundings which are conducive to my well-being and effectiveness.

___I cultivate trusting, reliable and mutually beneficial relationships, personally and professionally.

___I possess the stamina required by the demands of my work and life.

___I feel a deep drive to collaborate in the healthy evolution of life. I use my endeavors (such as my role as leader) as avenues to contribute to health and sustainability.

___I use my creative power to produce results that are meaningful, beneficial and sustainable for me and others.

___I keep my titles, roles, perks, wealth and all other forms of power in perspective. I know that these are not the 'end game.'

___I factor the potential consequences of my actions ahead of time into my personal and leadership decisions.

___I have a higher purpose, vision and values that focus and fuel my choices (such as what I purchase, where I live, how I lead and so on). My purpose, vision and values guide the direction my life and leadership takes.

___I know how to live in the present moment and let go of future or past concerns.

___I hold positive expectations for my future. I am optimistic.

___I appreciate life's profoundness, mysteries and ironies, and I allow these to remind me of the larger context in which I exist.

_____I am surrounded by people who candidly give me both appreciative and improvement feedback. They are a source of 'reality checking' for me.

_____I regularly practice some form of self-reflection so that I continuously manage and moderate my pursuits.

_____I am able to draw from both my internal and external resources in order to progress toward my goals.

_____I exercise my strengths rather than manage to my weaknesses to generate excellence in my life and work.

_____I have compassion for the human condition and the complex situations in which humanity finds itself.

_____I act decisively and courageously when the situation warrants.

_____I look for fundamental and sustainable solutions to recurring problems instead of reacting to the same problem over and over again.

_____I know how to quiet my mind in order to listen to a deeper wisdom. I bring this wisdom into my leadership decisions.

_____I actively contribute to a cause, a mission, a drive or relationships that generate wellth beyond my benefit.

_____I actively use my health and well-being to function at my optimal as a leader.

TOTAL SCORE [   ]

My Personal Wellth Quotient

Rating Scale:

135-150 Excellent!!

You have a knack for using attitudes and behaviors for health and well-being as a primary resource to effectively lead a life and work of wellth. Keep it up! You are a terrific role model for others. In fact, you may be a wonderful guide for other leaders who want to become more wellth-directed.

115-134 Good!!

You have a strong foundation on which to build. Determine how you can consciously use your health-oriented attitudes and behaviors as a potent resource for wellth in your life and leadership.

90-114 Doing Okay.

You may be risking effectiveness in your leadership and your life due to lack of attention to health-conscious attitudes and behaviors. Assess one to three areas that you are motivated to start strengthening today.

Below 90 Needs Attention!!

You are compromising your effectiveness by not paying attention to attitudes and behaviors for health and sustainability. Reflect on how your lack of health may negatively affect your leadership and your life. Choose one area that you will focus on to make improvements.

How Do You Get There from Here?

This book challenges you to generate wellth in *how* you lead so that you enrich the quality of results no matter *where* you lead. It calls you to hold a higher vision for your leadership, a profound compassion for human challenges and a passion for advancing greater wholeness and effectiveness in everything you do. It encourages you to create an ecology of wellth in your decisions and an economy of wellth for your company and the world.

You are not alone in pursuing wellth. In today's business complexity, wellth-driven leadership is a response gaining momentum and strength across the globe.

So, how do you learn to better generate wellth? *The 7 Essentials*[sm] framework, described in Chapter 5, is a decision-making tool that can help. You'll use it to bridge the gap from where you are now toward wellth-generating ideas and practices that fit your situation.

At least three types of people benefit from this framework. You may see yourself in one or all three:

1 - **The Enthusiast:** You are already driven to generate wellth. *The 7 Essentials,*[sm] then, enable you to further sharpen your decision-making skills so that you increase the positive impacts to your life, your business and the world.

2 - **The Pragmatist:** You are convinced that you want to step into a kind of 21st century, wellth-driven leadership that fits your style and presence. *The 7 Essentials*[sm] is a practical tool to help you architect the kind of business, social or personal wellth that matters to you most.

3 - **The Squeezed:** You feel pressured by the unending challenges you face. Learning *The 7 Essentials*[sm] gives you a fresh perspective on these pressures, and it suggests a few tips for creatively finding your way out. If you gain even a little relief, then it's worth your time and energy.

Regardless of where you start, *The 7 Essentials*^{sm} equips you to make clearer, more wellth-driven decisions to handle your 21st century leadership challenges and generate healthier possibilities.

Before diving into *The 7 Essentials,*^{sm} however, we first explore the question: *Why is it often difficult to sustain wellth-driven results?* Many leaders struggle to produce greater health and effectiveness to no avail. Initiating wellth-centered activities is usually not a problem. Why, then, is it tough to *sustain* positive, wellth-driven change? This is the topic of Chapter 4.

Chapter Highlights

- *Wellth is the progressive 21st century leadership drive to achieve and, more importantly, sustain results in the healthiest way possible. It is the cornerstone of the contemporary redefinition of the world, the new vanguard of consumers, workers and leaders from all walks of life who are crafting a more authentic, life-centric existence.*

- *The principle of wellth is just as applicable to your whole life, your relationships and your business success.*

- The 7 Essentials^{sm} *offers a bridge 21st century leaders can use to start leading and living a wellth-driven life. This decision-making framework, outlined in Chapter 5, provides a healthy approach to help you achieve and sustain meaningful, powerful results.*

the sustainability riddle

"...[the] failure to sustain significant change recurs again and again despite substantial resources committed to the change effort (many are bankrolled by top management), talented and committed people "driving the change," and high stakes. In fact, executives feeling an urgent need for change are right: companies that fail to sustain significant change end up facing crises. By then, their options are greatly reduced, and even after heroic efforts they often decline. ...the sources of these problems cannot be remedied by more expert advice, better consultants, or more committed managers. The sources lie in our most basic ways of thinking. ...we need to think less like managers and more like biologists." [1]

The Dance of Change

... global businesses are the first on the front line to really see and know the state of human rights in different parts of the world. ...Because global businesses are on the ground everywhere, they know that they have a choice. ...They can work to improve conditions, encouraging progress and more respect for individuals. Or they can ignore the issue. To be sure, businesses may not do badly if they take the latter option. Apathy and indifference—toward employees, consumers and communities—is often perceived to be synonymous with efficiency and competitiveness. But I believe that view is doomed to failure. Unless global corporations help improve local communities, the result will be a poorly educated workforce, a fundamental and worsening imbalance between haves and have-nots, social tension and an unproductive local economy. That is hardly a good prescription for long-term business success. ... It's good business for global companies to refuse to either take the easy road to quick, unsustainable profit, or bury their heads in the sand. ... I believe businesses have both a moral and commercial obligation to help be part of the solution." [2]

Doug Daft, CEO, The Coca-Cola Company

the sustainability riddle

why our efforts to sustain wellth-driven change
often fail dramatically

*Despite our best intentions, why doesn't
anything ever change around here?*

Didn't we take care of that problem already?

Why do we keep reinventing the wheel?

*We finally achieved the results that inspired us,
so why do we feel so exhausted?*

Perhaps nothing is more confounding to 21st century leaders
than finding a better way to maintain the positive results in which they've
invested their minds, hearts and resources. Especially when leaders know that
the ability to *sustain* healthy results is crucial in order to keep an organization
and its stakeholders prosperous.

What's even more perplexing is that no one has completely solved the
sustainability riddle. There's no one right answer that fits all situations. No
leader, no organization, no society has the *Holy Grail* we're looking for. There
are frameworks, like *The 7 Essentials*,[sm] that guide our thinking and decisions,
but we have to apply every framework to each circumstance individually.

Today, even the word *sustainability* is in the middle of an identity crisis.
Sustainability is often a proxy for environmental management, product
stewardship, cost reduction, corporate responsibility, economic development
and other activities,[3] a variety of notions which makes the subject confusing.
Bewildering as it seems, however, the new sustainability lingo signals

a positive trend: leaders are starting to grasp the profound relationship business has with the world around it. Leaders are beginning to respect that company practices which yield an unsustainable world eventually boomerang to yield unsustainable industries and businesses.

Nevertheless, most leaders aren't sure how to consistently turn *sustainability* initiatives, or any other kind of initiatives, into healthy and sustained value, or *wellth*. (No wonder so many companies end up with well-defined eco-management systems that produce very little real impact!) This is usually because, like most of us, leaders can hold faulty perceptions about how people and organizations *sustain* generative change.

> Leaders are starting to grasp the profound relationship business has with the world around it. They are beginning to respect that company practices which yield an unsustainable world eventually boomerang to yield unsustainable industries and businesses.

21st century leaders are realizing that the old paradigms which steer most change activities may be flawed, or, at the very least, limited. New initiatives are often implemented using mechanistic rather than systemic approaches. Like driving a nail into wood, the initiative is hammered into the organization's life without respect for how the organization digests change. As a result, the best, most wellth-intentioned efforts end up unsustained.

21st century leaders want better ways to achieve constructive results. They describe sustainability as the ability to make decisions and produce value that's both beneficial and self-perpetuating. They want to produce sustainable wellth. So, 21st century leaders reexamine their basic assumptions about how to *sustain* healthy change. The fallout of unsustainable change is just too toxic.

The Fallout of Unsustainable Change

As the following stories illustrate, we are plagued with the riddle of how to sustain healthy change in our organizations, our nations and our personal lives.

Within eight years the organization had at least six different leaders, each with the perfect 'fix' to solve the department's productivity issues. Among the array of fixes were new job descriptions for every employee, updated workflow diagrams and a twice-reengineered organizational structure. Each leader served the division long enough to stir things up before it was time to move on, so it should have been no surprise that by the end of eight years, productivity had gone from bad to worse.

Yes, each leader had the best intent. But no leader arrives to a clean slate. While the organization was scrambling to incorporate changes from one leader, the next leader architected new changes to boot. In a department overwhelmed by change, nothing had a positive and lasting effect. An incredible amount of time, money and enthusiasm was wasted, and the employees became uncaring and unresponsive to customers, to the department's goals and to each other. *How could the best laid plans create such mediocrity?*

Sustainability is the ability to make decisions and produce value that's beneficial and self-perpetuating.

Jerry's goal was to lose the bothersome pounds around his waistline in order to improve his physical health. He tried a high protein diet, then high carbohydrate, then wheat-free, then one-day-a-week fasting. Each diet had the same effect: some weight loss in the beginning of the program that stalled out after a few weeks. In fact, over time Jerry was starting to gain weight, contrary to his goal. He was at a loss about what to do. *How could a seemingly reasonable strategy for health produce the opposite effect from what was intended?*

Anti-Chinese riots raged in the streets of Jakarta in 1998. In reaction, government controls became severe. This was ironic, since for the almost 20 years prior, Indonesia had opened its doors to a free market economy in efforts to expand social and economic benefits to its citizens. Yet, the minority elite—mostly wealthy Chinese—disproportionately enjoyed the financial rewards that free market activity brought. The Indonesian majority was left with rising unemployment, dismal living conditions, poverty

"An achievement, no matter how magnificent, will eventually decay if not preserved by constant care." [4]
George Sheehan, columnist and athlete

and mounting hatred for their plight. Their anger erupted in widespread violence particularly aimed at the minority Chinese, and was answered by tighter central rule, contrary to the country's original goals.[5] *How could free market efforts, ostensibly for the better, trigger such widespread turmoil?*

Three accounts, each remarkably different on the surface. Look closely though. An unmistakable thread weaves through these real-life stories: *consciously sustaining healthy change is something we can learn to do better.* This thread zigzags across geographies, goals and gender. We are generally good at kicking off change and particularly motivated by heartfelt changes for the positive. However, as 21st century leaders, partnerships, organizations and societies, we have plenty of room to learn how to make wellth-directed changes that last rather than backfire. Clearly, we need greater wisdom about the process of change itself.

Consciously sustaining healthy change is something we can learn to do better.

All of us have experienced the toxic fallout of one unsustainable change or another:

- Initiatives we started long ago seem increasingly irrelevant as our realities (and we) evolve

- Human, financial and natural resources become exhausted through the change process

- An incompetence for handling the future becomes more apparent in individuals and groups who are stuck in the past

- People assume a 'this too shall pass' mentality, choosing not to pay attention to the next change that comes their way

- Resentment, fear, resistance or indifference swells within the various factions affected by change

- Blame, mistrust and isolation escalates as change divides rather than joins people

- Leaders at the highest levels seem to have an automatic reflex to revert to traditional ways of governing and decision-making when things get tough

- People feel a lack of purpose and personal fulfillment, along with the yearning to find greener pastures elsewhere

This kind of fallout is all too common. It actually opposes the changes we are trying to make. It's also predictable, especially when we don't factor in the indispensable lessons about how systems naturally sustain change (as well as how they don't!)

Indispensable Lessons for Sustaining Change

One of the primary roles of 21st century leaders is to generate the changes that lead whole systems toward a higher quality of operating, as well as added capacities to produce results that are healthy and sustainable. 21st century leaders perform this role every day. They attempt to shift a myriad of systems for the better, including markets, cities, companies, teams, employees, families and their personal lives. 21st century leaders are *systems architects*; a great deal of their work is to design and reinforce generative activities in systems of all shapes and sizes.

However, *forcing* a system to change often causes just the opposite: the system's *resistance*. This kind of resistance isn't a personal attack, although it frequently feels like one. This resistance is a hardwired reflex of a system that's provoked from how it's accustomed to behaving.

Individual consumers, groups and whole cultures show similar responses to outside efforts to modify their behavior. This means a person ordered to obey a new public law will likely react in the same manner as a city that undertakes an urban renewal project. We can adapt to change and we can resist it. Both of these responses are integral to our design, waiting to be triggered.

We can adapt to change and we can resist it. Both of these responses are integral to our design, waiting to be triggered.

Ironically, we forget that we're hardwired for adaptation *and* resistance. We assume that if a change makes sense rationally, it should be implemented trouble-free. We fall prey to the same unproductive traps that thwart our change efforts time and time again. Our best intentions regularly stop short of their longer-term promise.

To architect a wellth-driven change in behavior that endures, there are a few lessons to know in advance: [6,7,8,9]

- **The harder you push, the harder the system pushes back.**

  Our common answer to resolve a problem is to *work harder to fix it* and to *hit the problem head on*. We push and push to make change happen. For instance, if working longer hours today gets the work done, then a strategy for working longer hours every day must be better! (Right?) While aggressive tactics, like working long hours, often succeed in the short run, they have inherent limitations. They burn out our energy and resources; therefore, they are not sustainable over time. Plus, they kick off a natural response in the system to *push back* in order to maintain its status quo. For example, our strategy to work longer results in stress and fatigue that squash our desire to work at all! By pushing the system harder to change, we inadvertently cause the system to muster its energies to stay the same, or worse, to go in the opposite direction.

- **Familiar solutions usually reinforce the problem.**

  In business, as in life, we tend to be most comfortable when we apply what we know best, such as the familiar solutions that worked in the past. But that can get us into trouble if we presume a new situation is identical to situations we've been in before. What's more insidious is that our old solutions may appear to work in the short term but may actually make our situation worse over time. For instance, we cut headcount in response to our company's diving market share, without realizing that little by little we're eating away at the company's capability to innovate. Or, we drink alcohol to ease our frustrations, only to find that we mistakenly hurt our relationships by drinking too much. When we get addicted to familiar solutions, our problems get worse, and we undermine our ability to fix them.

- **Faster is slower.**

  All systems have optimal rates of growth, and these are usually far less than the fastest growth possible. In fact, the fastest growth possible is usually growth that's *out of control*. For example, an athlete can take steroids to rapidly hyper-develop her physique, but not without traumatizing her liver and causing wild swings in her moods. By trying to change too much too quickly, she's injured her competitiveness today and her health for a lifetime. To counterbalance change that's coming too fast, a healthy system will cause itself to slow down so that it can incorporate the change into its design. If not, the system is headed for irreparable damage.

- **Cause and effect aren't closely related in time and space.**

   Problems usually start because of actions a person or persons took long ago. There is a delay between the initial causes and their systemic effects, a period of time we rarely factor into our plans. Conceptually, this sounds logical, yet when push comes to shove, most of us act like our problems appeared out of thin air or because of something recent. We assume that cause and effect are closely related, and, to solve our problems we choose solutions that are easiest to find. Frequently, these are the exact solutions that *exacerbate* the problem. Without knowing the deeper reasons our problems came to be in the first place, our changes are neither fundamental nor sustainable.

- **Small actions can produce big results.**

   Because all systems are interconnected and influence each other, small actions of one system can ripple into big impact elsewhere. The positive and negative consequences of an action spread circuitously, instead of one linear step at a time. This process isn't in our control. More puzzling, it's hard to know which of our actions will most likely favor the results we want. All we can do is take action as mindfully as we can, and stay open and accountable to the outcomes our actions produce.

- **Complex problems have more than one right answer.**

  Sometimes we get stuck trying to resolve an issue because we're hunting for the *one perfect answer,* as if all other options are wrong. This is a lot like searching for a needle in a haystack! Complex problems are caused by the interplay of wide-ranging influences, such as our upbringing, social and political institutions, our relationships and our personal beliefs. Because most problems are systemic and multifaceted, many roads can generate energy for sustained change. We're never limited to just one solution.

- **There is no blame because there is no 'them.'**

  An easy way to feel better about a problem is to lay blame for it somewhere—on senior leadership, on the sales force, on a co-worker, on a spouse, on our children. Business is the root of the world's ills; commercials are the reason we eat too much; a particular group of people is the sole cause of violence. But in actuality there is no one faction to blame for most problems. Problems emanate from the interaction of a host of thoughts and actions taken by people and institutions over time. No one person or thing is the cause; we all contribute to the problem in some way, whether by commission or omission. Furthermore, hurling blame towards others isn't a productive way out. The more we blame others, the more defensive they are likely to become and the less likely we are to realize productive change.

Clearly, the strategies we frequently use to sustain wellth-oriented change cause more problems than those strategies alleviate. The list above helps us understand the patterns that trigger resistance so that we don't sabotage our wellth-seeking progress.

21st Century Leadership in Action:
Diagnosing a Problem Using a Systems View

Choose a problem that you are attempting to resolve. Based on the bullets above, diagnose your change strategies by asking the following questions:

- *Am I pushing too hard or too directly on the system to resolve this problem? How might the system compensate to stay as it is?*

- *Am I applying old or familiar solutions to this problem? What is the same about this situation, and what might be different? What new options can I consider?*

- *Am I trying to address this problem with quick, short-term solutions? How might these solutions slow me down or hurt my effectiveness in the long run?*

- *What appears to be the obvious cause of the problem? What deeper causes could be contributing to it?*

- *Am I trying to resolve this problem by applying a lot of resources, such as time, energy, money, etc.? Am I overwhelming the system with these resources? Alternatively, what small actions might I take to better use these resources as well as have a better impact?*

- *Am I seeing my options for resolving this problem as an either/or choice? How can I generate other solutions to give me more latitude and freedom?*

- *Am I blaming someone or something else for my problem? Who or what do I believe is inhibiting me or my problem-solving efforts? How might I be contributing to this problem with my thinking and actions?*

Based on your answers to these questions, consider alternative approaches you can take to better understand your problem and make sustained progress to solve it.

The 7 Essentials, outlined in Chapter 5, provides 21st century leaders a fresh, integral way of progressing toward the results they want in order to make a difference in the sustainability of results they actually get.

A New Way to Think about Growth

No question, generating wellth requires change, whether that change is incremental or radical, modest or far-reaching, internally felt or externally seen. Most of us realize that. What we frequently forget is that to sustain a wellth-directed change over time (like a better habit, a new capability or a healthier measure of success), we must genuinely appreciate and work with the innate growth tendencies of healthy systems rather than attempt to override them.

To sustain a wellth-directed change over time we must genuinely appreciate and work with the innate growth tendencies of healthy systems rather than attempt to override them.

In a nutshell, change requires that we grow, and to grow means to shift from the results we are getting now to the results we want. Strangely, we usually assume that growth will happen immediately. We even expect the returns of our change efforts should get better and better in a nonstop fashion:

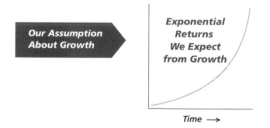

Our Assumption About Growth

Exponential Returns We Expect from Growth

Time →

We expect everything to grow exponentially—to get larger, better, faster—like clockwork. Business profits should go up every quarter, our careers should keep rising and even the intelligence of our kids should improve without fail. If not, something is terribly wrong. We measure success using a few narrowly-defined variables, like profit, without addressing the hidden costs of pushing for a kind of growth we can't possibly sustain. No healthy system can. And, to make matters worse, we don't question that our logic about growth may be deeply flawed.

| Our Company's Quarterly Profits | My Career Progression | My Kid's Intelligence |

We use the same assumption about growth in every arena of life

What we don't realize, but can learn from studying nature, is that healthy living systems evolve and sustain greater capability, well-being and results in a rhythm of highs and lows. Check your personal experience on this. The profits of a company are marked by ups and downs, career growth is scattered with dry spells, and kids naturally learn at a rhythm that makes sense for them individually.

On the other hand, living systems which grow unrestrained are completely out of whack. The rampant spread of cancer is one example. Something in the body runs amuck, the first of many signs that the person is ill.

An impossibly high bar has been set for CEOs and their companies to produce unmitigated double-digit growth. Yet, research by Dr. John Kotter of Harvard Business School shows that "earnings are unlikely to grow faster than GDP [Gross Domestic Product] for more than short periods ... Moreover, most companies jog along at much the same pace as the rest of their industry most of the time."[10] We've created a pressurized system that demands double-digit growth, yet that kind of growth clearly isn't reinforced by the economy nor is it sustainable. In fact, the rapid demise of so many

companies in recent years has taught us: the system we've designed for the sake of high stakes, short-term profit can breed unethical decisions and detrimental results.

In living systems, whether a flourishing rose bush or a community of rabbits, growth actually looks more like this:[11]

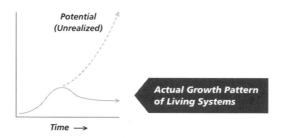

This graph doesn't just reflect a pattern in the natural world; it also reflects what happens when people attempt to grow and change. It follows the s-shaped curve that characterizes the evolution of life. Growth accelerates then slows as the living system fully matures.

The conditions in which the system exists simultaneously encourage and limit the process of growth. In this way, "…every movement is being inhibited as it occurs."[12] As a result, for healthy and sustained growth, it is crucial to work *equally* with the forces to catalyze a change as well as the forces to stabilize it. Working with both these forces enables the system to evolve new capabilities to meet the demands of its changing circumstances.

In this light, the 21st century leader's role isn't just to kick off wellth-oriented change; it is also about doing what it takes to make sure the change has staying power. Appreciating how to catalyze *and* sustain change is a critical balance 21st century leaders have to work through to make a meaningful, enduring difference.

Like a parent who promotes the right environment for a child's development or a farmer who tills the soil to produce a rich field of corn, 21st century leaders must first discover what conditions will build momentum for their change effort. At this stage, any limits that might bring the change to a stall must also be addressed and, when possible, managed. Limits to growth, such as cultural norms, laws, natural resources, money, creative capital and the like, are not bad per se; they are the natural boundaries that become clearer and clearer with every action that's taken to move ahead.

Once a change effort gains momentum of its own, the act of sustaining it requires a shift in the 21st century leader's strategy. Reinforcing the momentum is still important. Yet, limiting forces can now be proactively used to solidify a new order, harmony and stability.

The "biological world teaches that sustaining change requires understanding the reinforcing growth processes and what is needed to catalyze them, and addressing the limits that keep change from occurring."[13]

While many companies have their eye solely on profit, one company stands apart from the pack. Merck & Company, a global pharmaceutical business, actively uses *ethics* to manage business growth. When, in a strategic planning meeting, a group of executives were asked what they do to consciously manage growth, three hands immediately shot up. "We use our ethics and values!" was their first response. Merck operates from a +100-year-old ethical foundation to drive its research programs, direct the manufacture and sales of its drugs, guide its partnerships and generate sustained growth for the company and societies worldwide. In fact, in two separate 2002 studies of global companies and the pharmaceutical industry, Merck was internationally rated most ethical not just in its policies, but in how it gets results.[14]

Consciously-designed limits, such as applying clear principles and infrastructure to support a particular change, can help the system internalize new attitudes and skills so that it arrives at a healthier equilibrium. In essence, the system is arriving at a whole new way of operating.

By simply understanding change initiatives from the perspective of living systems, 21st century leaders find more strategic questions that they couldn't ask before:

To *start* the change initiative –

What conditions may build momentum for the results we want?
How will we naturally optimize those conditions?

What conditions may limit the results we want?
How will we respect and address those conditions?

To *sustain* the change initiative –

What conditions may sustain the results we want?
How will we use those conditions to transform the change into a healthy and stable mode of operating?

Right from the start, these questions enable 21st century leaders to proactively design and promote circumstances that favor healthier, longer-lasting success.

Chapter 5 uses *The 7 Essentials*^{sm} to further explain the dynamics of healthy, sustainable change, and how you can apply this framework to make wellth-driven decisions.

How 21st Century Leaders Steward Healthy, Sustainable Change

21st century leaders aren't concerned with influencing random change. They steward changes that improve the health and effectiveness of people, businesses and the larger natural and social world. For instance, 21st century leaders:

- Implement eco-friendly manufacturing processes and technologies
- Transform social difficulties, such as the digital divide or worldwide malnutrition, into social and business profit
- Use pricing structures that account for social and environmental costs of their business practices
- Engage in industries that advance the evolution of humanity
- Shape consumers' lives with marketing messages that are conscientious, truthful and educational
- Sponsor transparent audits of their financial, social and environmental performance
- Use their aspirations, deeper purpose, core values and company strengths to regulate their strategies for business growth
- Provide safe, legal and healthy working conditions and cultivate a wellth-driven business culture
- Use corporate power in ways that promote healthy and sustainable leadership practices in the larger geopolitical and economic arenas

In effect, 21st century leaders are driven to protect and promote new degrees of sustainable wellth wherever they can.

A different orientation allows 21st century leaders to succeed in sustaining their wellth-driven change efforts. These leaders are more apt to regard *wholes* rather than parts, *influence and partner* rather than intervene or force, *balance short and long-term objectives* rather than succumb to immediate pressures, and *create with a natural momentum* for change rather than merely react to resistance.

21st century leaders strive to produce change that is wellth-directed and self-perpetuating.

Plus, their life-centric values remind 21st century leaders that life is all about change. Life is impermanent, fluid and unfolding to new possibilities. No moment is the same as the next. Individuals, teams, nature and society are already constantly changing. In truth, these systems *must* change if they are to be vibrant and function well. 21st century leaders see their job as generating the environments and structures that promote the self-determination and collaborative evolution of healthy systems everywhere.

21st century leaders naturally take a wider outlook throughout the change process. You can adopt this outlook in your change efforts as well, starting with the following actions:

- **Choose wellth-driven change.** Select change efforts that generate positive, meaningful and relevant results for the system with which you work, such as a team, your business or a culture. Help the system connect to a deeply felt aspiration that's worth changing for, something to believe in that compels the system to *want* to shift to a healthier form of success. Chapter 3 can support you in discussing this kind of wellth-driven change with others.

> **What is the most stressful condition a person can face? "Not having something to believe in."[15]**
>
> Hans Selye, pioneer in stress research

- **Forecast the consequences.** Consider the short and longer-term impacts that the change may have to multiple stakeholders, such as your company, workforce, business partners, the environment, vendors and other alliances. Factor these potential consequences into your plans for change, staying aligned with the intent to do good rather than harm.

- **Assess the readiness for change.** Check to see if people are generally free of problems that would distract them from the goals of the change. Plus, find out if they are open to wholly new solutions rather than attached to traditional approaches that could prevent progress. Ensure people are committed to the time, dedication and resources required for the change to succeed over the long haul. It may help to share the natural dynamics of change described in this chapter so that everyone is ready for the rollercoaster of ups and downs that are part and parcel of the change process.

- **Determine your role in the change effort.** Figure out how you can be a constructive and enabling influence. Chapter 6 can help you uncover the purpose, values and strengths to guide you. A clear purpose, values and strengths will help you bring the best of your leadership and whole health into your role so that you perform your responsibilities effortlessly and sustainably.

- **Cultivate the system's capabilities.** Assist the system you are working with to contribute to its own change. Your job isn't to 'fix' the system as an all-knowing, all-seeing expert. That would not only be impossible; it would also create unsustainable dependencies on you. As this chapter explains, your job is to enable the system to solve its own problems and grow healthier results ultimately without your guidance or resources.

> "The evidence seems clear that those businesses which actively serve their many constituencies in creative, morally thoughtful ways also, over the long run, serve their shareholders best. Companies do, in fact, do well by doing good."[16]
>
> Norman Lear, Chairman and CEO, Act III Communications and Founder of Business Enterprise Trust

- **Ask strategic questions.** Strategic questions open up new possibilities and deepen the system's wisdom of itself. These kinds of questions also ensure that people are concentrated around the right challenges and wellth-driven aspirations rather than changing out of stress or fear. Chapter 7 assists you in how to ask healthy, strategic questions using *The 7 Essentials*^{sm} framework.

- **Listen deeply.** Listen deeply to the nature of the system—the person or team or culture with which you are working (especially yourself!) Every living system has qualities that define what it needs for good health and sustainable performance. And, every system has a built-in drive for growth along with limitations. The act of changing puts demands on the system; the system will respond by stopping short of its potential, resisting the change or learning how to flourish in new circumstances. Pay attention to how the system works to inform you in how best to support it.

- **Influence and let go.** Strive to generatively *influence* the change process, but let go of control. By design, a living system *cannot* be externally controlled *and* fully thrive at the same time. This puts you in a more humble, facilitative role and shows great respect for the system.

- **Apply standardized tools as appropriate.** Utilize tools and methods for change only to the extent of their usefulness. Human and natural systems are too unique for any one-size-fits-all format, and we are simply too ignorant about the full complexities of these systems. Technologies, such as change management techniques, are valuable guides, but they cannot be imposed in the same way on every living system every time.

- **Balance wellth-driven growth with sustainability.** Help people in the system consciously manage the pursuit of their change goals by: 1) identifying the internal and external barriers to change as well as ways to rectify these barriers, plus 2) exercising the values, structures and practices that lead to a healthier, more mindful and confident way of functioning. You'll be better equipped to do this by helping people apply the elements of Integrity outlined in Chapter 6.

Much can be learned about creating wellth by 21st century leaders and businesses that are already doing it, such as GrameenPhone.

GrameenPhone was launched in 1997 to provide mobile phone services in Bangladesh. The company had a clear mission: to generate economic and social benefit through communication technologies. This would prove to be a considerable change for Bangladesh.

Instead of forcing its way into this new market as other firms might have, the company spent time understanding the indigenous values, circumstances, networks of influence and aspirations. This gentler approach helped GrameenPhone partner with the country and a range of investors. Plus, GrameenPhone was better able to create locally-relevant avenues to channel capital, infrastructure and education directly to people who could influence business and social results (in this case, community-based women entrepreneurs.) Entrepreneurs were enabled to buy cellular handsets with loans from microcredit pioneer Grameen Bank, and then rent the phones with airtime to neighbors.

Through their community networks, women entrepreneurs organically spread GrameenPhone's product far and wide, enhancing the sales, economic wealth and communication services in the region. Today, GrameenPhone has "nearly 1 million direct subscribers in addition to the 30,000 entrepreneurs whose handsets provide phone access to 50 million people." Now, Bangladesh's largest phone company, GrameenPhone reached profits of $44 million in 2002.

The story gets better. Iqbal Quadir, GrameenPhone's founder, always saw profits not as the end, but as the means to expand the company's services, reward investors and generate social good. Today, more and more of GrameenPhone's entrepreneurs use their newfound wealth to improve the well-being of their families and communities. Feeling a larger sense of empowerment, they also push for political, social and educational reforms in Bangladesh.

GrameenPhone's approach to change is said best by Quadir: "...investing in local entrepreneurs, rather than funneling aid to their governments, may be the best hope for the world's developing economies." In part, through the conscious business strategies of GrameenPhone, democratic and other positive reforms have greater potential to take root.[17]

A wellth-centric approach to change adds a fundamentally new mindset, set of questions and approaches to the 21st century leadership toolkit. It requires 21st century leaders to learn how to use life's energy in order to help sustain powerful results.

However, this approach is not just about how to use life to serve self-centered purposes. It is also about producing results that add value to life as well. Instead of wasting time trying to control life, 21st century leaders create a generative collaboration with life and its evolutionary processes.

Detailed in Chapter 5, *The 7 Essentials*^{sm} framework suggests that there are at least seven dynamics to be aware of when cultivating healthy, systemic and sustainable change. Altogether, these seven essentials provide a new lens from which to make 21st century leadership decisions in concert with a life-enhancing approach for achieving results. When you use *The 7 Essentials*,^{sm} you are more apt to design wholeness, conscious growth and integrated results into your change process. That is, you are more likely to achieve progressive, sustainable wellth.

Chapter Highlights

- *Most leaders aren't sure how to consistently turn their initiatives into sustained value, or what we call* wellth. *This is usually because leaders often hold faulty perceptions about how people and organizations make and sustain generative change.*

- *21st century leaders want better ways to achieve and sustain results in their lives, organizations and worldwide. They describe* sustainability *as* the ability to make decisions and produce value that's both beneficial and self-perpetuating, *the ability to produce sustainable wellth.*

- *Forcing a system to change often causes just the opposite: resistance to change. This resistance is a hardwired reflex of a system that's provoked from how it's accustomed to behaving. We can learn from these reflexive patterns in order to sustain healthy change.*

- *By simply seeing our change initiatives from the perspective of nature, 21st century leaders better understand the conditions that reinforce the results they want and those conditions that don't. These leaders strive to promote the circumstances that favor healthier, longer-lasting success in all their change efforts, personally and professionally.*

the 7 essentials^{sm}

"A human being is part of the Whole...He experiences himself, his thoughts and feelings, as something separated from the rest...a kind of optical delusion of his consciousness. This delusion is a kind of prison for us, restricting us to our personal desires and to affection for a few persons nearest us. Our task must be to free ourselves from this prison by widening our circle of compassion to embrace all living creatures and the whole of nature in its beauty. Nobody is able to achieve this completely, but the striving for such achievement is, in itself, a part of the liberation and a foundation for inner security".[1]

Albert Einstein, physicist

the 7 essentials^{sm}

a dynamic tool 21st century leaders use to generate
healthy and sustainable results

In previous chapters we talked about the values leading a movement
of consumers, workers and businesses alike to choose greater health and
effectiveness on all fronts. We also discussed a new kind of 21st century
leader and why this leadership is vital in order to successfully respond to the
health-conscious value system emerging today.

We explored the idea of *wellth* as the innate drive of 21st century leaders,
mature people who are driven to advance initiatives and organizations
to benefit life now and for generations to come. Being realistic, we also
addressed a significant conundrum: if most leaders are willing to initiate
positive changes for greater wellth, then why are those changes frequently
difficult to sustain?

The focus of this chapter is *The 7 Essentials,*^{sm} a valuable decision-making
tool that can help you not only kick off generative change but also sustain it. This
tool aids 21st century leaders to achieve goals in a wellth-driven manner.

The 7 Essentials^{sm}

The 7 Essentials^{sm} is a system of principles integral to the process of cultivating
healthy results. It consists of seven distinct, yet interrelated essentials:
Integrity, Aspiration, Innovation, Movement, Simplicity, Sustainability and
Renewal. In total, this system reminds you to consciously choose your
strategies for personal and business growth so that you experience greater
health by way of your actions.

The 7 Essentials^{sm} is a model for producing results that stems from a
fundamentally different core than most results-based models. With it, you

address complex problems more holistically, and become better equipped to operate with wellth-driven approaches. The net effect is that you channel your 21st century leadership power into more compelling questions, decisions and accomplishments.

As you'll discover in this chapter, the model is purposefully non-linear to better cope with the dynamic complexities of modern life. It is a thinking device, offering a whole new way of seeing so that you discover healthier solutions to your challenges. Plus, it's a decision-making tool that puts forward the strategic questions which can transform your unique problem or situation into one of immense opportunity and learning.

The 7 Essentials^{sm} is a system of seven distinct, yet interrelated principles integral to the process of cultivating healthy results: Integrity, Aspiration, Innovation, Movement, Simplicity, Sustainability and Renewal.

This framework is not an answer in itself. It's a bridge you can use time and time again to reach answers on your own. It is a truth, but not The Truth. It's a useful instrument that enables you to clarify, achieve and uphold wellth-driven results more progressively and responsibly. Like all tools, its utility and value greatly depend on the enthusiasm and discipline that you put into using it.

The Core Question of *The 7 Essentials*^{sm}

The 7 Essentials^{sm} is a mechanism for intentionally creating results that improve the viability of life—for the world, for your efforts and for your self. We've used this framework most often with business leaders who are executives, directors, line managers and entrepreneurs. However, it can be applied in any situation, business or otherwise, where you want to accomplish results in a better and simpler manner than you've done before.

In fact, the core question that this framework asks you to answer is:

How can success be achieved and sustained in a healthy, life-enhancing way?

This question is inherently wellth-directed. It urges you to generate results from a creative orientation rather than a reactive one, ease rather than willpower, harmony rather than resistance, with the whole rather than just your self or your business in mind.

We believe that this question is foremost in the line of inquiry of 21st century leaders, no matter the arena in which they strive. This question applies similarly to the entrepreneur who plans for conscious business growth, the individual who adopts a new exercise routine, the executive team that addresses the broader costs of its business strategies and the city that strives for greater economic, social and environmental balance. 21st century leaders are determined to use methods, such as *The 7 Essentials*,^{sm} to participate in the creation of healthy results and healthy systems everywhere they are.

> For the 21st century leadership mind, health is the natural ability of any living entity, no matter how small or large, to thrive, given the conditions in which it exists.

What is a Healthy System?

Before diving into *The 7 Essentials*,^{sm} you may be wondering: *What is a healthy system?* Good question! For the 21st century leadership mind, the word *health* is the natural ability of any living entity, no matter how small or large, to thrive, given the conditions in which it exists. Health isn't just about survival. It isn't the absence of illness and disease. A healthy system —whether profit-making businesses, product teams or individual people—is an entity which meets these basic attributes:

- **Productive.** A healthy system functions effectively to fulfill its purpose given the circumstances in which it lives.

- **Adaptive.** As circumstances change and new challenges arise, a healthy system makes adjustments and responds resourcefully rather than letting challenges drain it.

- **Preventive.** A healthy system takes measures, whenever possible, to anticipate and resolve problems before they occur.

- **Supportive.** A healthy system sustains that which favors its health and success over the long-haul.

- **Integrative.** A healthy system brings together the unique purposes, values, strengths and relationships of differing parts of the system into a well-functioning whole that is more resilient than its parts.

- **Creative.** A healthy system proactively participates in shaping its future.

A healthy system is the only type of entity that evolves to meet and transcend its challenges, that is, to reinvent and maintain itself over time. It is self-determining and self-sustaining, yet always in the context of its relationships and limits. The quality of its well-being and performance affect the well-being and performance of the systems around it.

> **Patagonia is known for its determination to achieve and sustain healthy forms of business and ecological success. Michael Crooke, the company's CEO, goes so far to say that "to threaten the environment is to threaten existence." In the 1990s, the company put its values to a clear test: to recognize the enormous human and ecological consequences of using regular cotton and to shift to clothing and products that were entirely organic. This test was an upheaval for Patagonia; it meant educating the workforce about the nature of organic cotton, totally redesigning manufacturing processes and overhauling vendor relationships. The shift to organics also resulted in a plummet in sales from $70 million to $50 million, until the company transformation was complete. Nonetheless, Patagonia stuck with it, turning its values for health and sustainability into profitable business practice. Today, organic cotton is one of Patagonia's biggest selling points for consumers. The company literally re-shaped what's expected of the outdoor apparel industry.[2]**

21st century leaders employ technologies to cultivate healthy systems because these systems propagate healthier results. One of the technologies these leaders use is *The 7 Essentials.*[sm]

The Design of
The 7 Essentials^{sm}

The 7 Essentials^{sm} isn't merely intellectual theory nor is it the latest management fad. It reflects core patterns of human wisdom accumulated across a broad range of philosophies and sciences as well as the authors' years of practical experience facilitating the development of formal and informal leaders and groups of all shapes and sizes. In particular, the framework draws heavily on theories about what fosters healthy living systems, such as nature, and the application of these theories to people and business. (See "The Wisdom Underlying *The 7 Essentials*^{sm}" in the Appendix for more in-depth information.)

However, you don't need to get too theoretical to grasp the essence of *The 7 Essentials*^{sm} Each of us encounters and works with a range of living and dying systems everyday, such as our economies, our organizations, our families and our physical bodies. We have an unconscious knowledge about how to work with and within systems to get beneficial and sustained results. The goal of *The 7 Essentials*^{sm} is to make this knowledge conscious, and, therefore, a wellspring from which you can easily draw.

To understand the basic design of this framework, consider *The 7 Essentials*^{sm} as you would a tree. The wisdom underlying the model acts as the tree's roots, nourishing the growth of the framework so that it doesn't get stagnant. Consequently, the framework continually evolves as human beings learn more about how to consistently achieve and sustain healthy forms of success.

> "Until recently, businesspeople saw their worlds through the Industrial Age metaphor of the machine and built their organizations accordingly. Now, in irreversibly increasing numbers, they see business more as a living system. And in the process they are leading business back to its roots as a natural and fundamentally human institution." [3]
>
> Thomas Petzinger, Wall Street Journal reporter and author

The framework itself is like the trunk and the branches of the tree, the means for channeling energy and resources to some sort of outgrowth. This outgrowth, such as leaves and fruit, are the tree's results, what it's naturally designed to produce. An apple tree doesn't yield coconuts nor does the palm tree make apples. A certain type of tree is innately designed to produce something in particular. In the case of *The 7 Essentials^sm* framework, this something in particular is wellth.

As you can see from this tree metaphor, *The 7 Essentials^sm* is an aid to move more conscientiously from a deeper level of wisdom *about the world* to healthy results *in the world*. The model suggests that there are mechanisms we can use for advancing system-wide health as either the focal point or a by-product of producing other results.

The 7 Essentials^sm is an aid to move more conscientiously from a deeper level of wisdom about the world to healthy results in the world.

For instance, a pharmaceutical team can manufacture and sell a drug in ways that are less likely to compromise the environment or the health of the pharmaceutical industry. At every step of the drug's life cycle, the team can doggedly ask the question at the heart of *The 7 Essentials^sm*: *How can we achieve and sustain success in a healthy, life-enhancing way?* By making wellth-based decisions, the team can reap considerable, yet unexpected advantages, such as: a leadership team that's energized rather than exhausted when its time for the drug to go to market, business strategies that consider the longer-term effects on the environment once the drug is consumed, plus a positive reputation of the brand that attracts rather than displeases health-conscious consumers.

When we understand the whole tree and the relationships that constitute it, we better appreciate the cycle of growth, sustenance and renewal built into nature's design. Fruits and leaves nourish people, insects and animals. Likewise, *wellth-driven* business activities nourish benefits far beyond the initial returns for which they were designed. The tree—and all of nature— provides a completely new frame from which to understand the dynamics of business.

Just like a vibrant tree, humans are always in the middle of creating something; we are endowed with the capability to *create*. The 21st century stretch is for us to intentionally direct our creative capability toward experiences and things that foster health and sustainability. *The 7 Essentials^sm* helps us do this.

The framework reflects how people, from individuals to whole societies, realize results *at the same time* they enhance personal and collective well-being. It highlights key capabilities we instinctively bring into play when we produce results that matter to us. Actively working with *The 7 Essentials*[sm] makes us more aware of our methods for generating healthy results so that we do so with greater ease, satisfaction and impact.

Each Essential:
A Facet of the Whole

See the aspen grove, the flock of birds, the children, the natural beauty outside your window? Thriving living systems are plentiful, available to teach us their wisdom if we only pay attention.

Life and its processes are still largely a mystery to humankind, yet there are some things we've learned. We know that, biologically speaking, long-lasting success for one form of life or another isn't a certainty; it's a possibility. Life appears to be emergent, generally evolving toward greater complexity and, consequently, constantly increasing its possibilities for survival and long-term success. Life has an evolutionary drive, or what some call an intrinsic creative intelligence.[4] *The 7 Essentials*[sm] is one way to mindfully work with this creative drive instead of against it.

With this framework, you gain an understanding about the intelligence life uses to evolve. Each essential is among the properties or core capabilities of dynamic and healthy living systems. You can access and apply this intelligence to produce results in a life-promoting manner. The key is the degree of consciousness you bring in doing so.

You can access and apply the intelligence of *The 7 Essentials*[sm] to produce results in a life-promoting manner. The key is the degree of consciousness you bring in doing so.

As consistent patterns derived from the study of nature, the essentials aren't bound by our biases. Like gravity which exists whether we name it or not, the essentials know no lack or limitation of their own.[5] How we experience the essentials is only restricted by our acceptance and use of them. As a result, the essentials can support you to reap bigger and better impact the moment you widen your thinking and deepen your application of them.

Each essential is a mechanism for asking mind-opening questions about how to generate results in health-seeking ways. The essentials re-direct our attention toward intentions and actions we may not have explored before.

This act of questioning alone releases a tremendous amount of creative energy that's usually pent-up or ignored. (You'll learn about the power of using *The 7 Essentials*^{sm} to ask transformative questions in Chapter 7.)

Although the essentials actually work in a coordinated system, each contains a distinctive facet of the whole. The following pages express the essentials as general principles; nevertheless, read them as if they were referring to what is going on in your world right now. If you do, you'll find they have the power to liberate your thinking to healthier assumptions for generating results.

Integrity

Latin root, *integritas*, meaning "soundness"

Definition: How a living system is naturally healthiest, most successful and whole

A healthy living system works in accordance to its natural design. It sustains the health of its elements, its relationships and its self as a whole.

A living system is in Integrity when all aspects of it work together synergistically, resulting in the health, good performance and sustainability of its parts as well as the system overall. Because of Integrity, the system experiences a quality of wholeness, a coherent role within its environment and a clarified ease in its interrelationships. In the language of *The 7 Essentials*^{sm} Integrity is a healthy system's most fundamental design component. (Chapter 6 will deepen your knowledge about Integrity and how to activate it in your leadership.)

A healthy living system works in harmony with its Integrity, not against it. A simple example: the heart is designed to pump and circulate blood. Lungs are designed to inhale, filter and exhale air. A heart cannot function as lungs, nor can lungs do the work of the heart, at least not without a tremendous amount of energy, stress and strain ... basically, a total transformation. The heart and lungs each have distinct purposes. Yet, heart and lungs are also highly interconnected. They are subsystems that support a common goal: the health of the human body. That human body, or an individual person, is a subsystem that's crucial to the effective functioning of larger systems, such as the person's family and community. Integrity is a vital principle for wellth at every level.

Aspiration

Latin root, *aspirare*, "to breathe"

Definition: How a living system generates results that matter to it

A healthy living system grows toward meaningful results.

A basic feature of a healthy living system, of life itself, is to grow toward particular results. With its Latin root *aspirare* meaning to breathe, the very word Aspiration suggests that the act of aspiring, or growing, is as indispensable to the well-being of life as breathing is.

In a healthy human system, like a community or a business, Aspiration takes on an added meaning: the ability to intentionally create something that we care about. To be human is to be a creator; giving birth to a vision or goal gives our lives significance and makes us feel alive.

We are inherently creative beings, motivated to seek projects where we can genuinely express our ideas and passions. From the ingenuity of a child who freely explores her world to entire social movements initiated by a small spirited group, through our creative acts the power of Aspiration fosters a sense of enthusiasm for life along with a final product, the creation.

Innovation

Latin root, *innovare*, *innovat*, "to introduce anew"

Definition: How a living system experiments and learns

*A healthy living system creatively experiments
to adapt to its changing conditions.*

Diversity, originality and learning are hallmarks of nature. Or, as physicist Fritjof Capra says, "Life constantly reaches out into novelty."[6] There are always new potentials, variations and iterations forming and reforming in every healthy living system. These systems have plasticity; to a degree often greater than imagined, living systems can restructure their design and function in response to disturbances in their environment. They are adaptive and innovative.

Innovation is how living systems break through existing constraints that, at times, may seem to undermine the health of the whole. But, this is only temporary. Productive innovations don't compromise the basic health and wholeness of the system over time; in fact, these innovations provoke the system to get better at handling the ever-changing conditions it's in. So, while in the short run, Innovation may cause systemic upset, in the long-run Innovation is absolutely required for sustained, system-wide success. Innovation is the energy that stimulates the system to evolve.

Movement

Latin root, *movimentum*, *movere*, "to move"

Definition: How a living system extends itself through action

A healthy living system directs its actions.

Movement is about purposeful energy flow to and from as well as within a living system. Whether as bouncing particles or circling planets, healthy living systems are always in active motion to some degree. Ants build, muscles contract, babies crawl. Movement is all about directed action and the lack of it leads to stagnation, one of the first signs the system is deteriorating. In fact, it is often through action, no matter how minuscule, that we are sure something is alive.

Through the influence of action, every system is connected to every other system, whether or not the connection is visible to the naked eye. Movement, then, is also about how systems act to share resources, communicate and cooperate with one another, the flows of energy and activity that are necessary for each system to stay alive and to thrive. "Life did not take over the planet by combat but by cooperation, partnership, and networking."[7]

Simplicity

Latin root, *simplicitas*, "absent of pretense"

Definition: How a living system uses
minimal energy to produce maximum effect

*A healthy living system knows how and
when to conserve its energy.*

Simplicity is how a living system conserves its energies. At the same time healthy living systems can diversify and experiment, they are also amazingly efficient. They know how to streamline their use of resources. Take, for instance, the tortoise's shell, an armor designed with a hexagon shape. This shape allows the tortoise to use a minimal amount of energy yet gain a maximum amount of strength and protection within its environment.[8]

Within even the most complex living system lies the capability of Simplicity, the mechanisms that reduce the system's workload for the effect to raise its chance for success.

Sustainability

Latin root, *sustinere*, "to hold up"

Definition: How a living system preserves
and builds on what it creates

*A healthy living system is resilient.
Because of its capabilities, its results have
long-lived staying power.*

A healthy living system demonstrates Sustainability when it adapts to challenges with alternatives and innovations that stick over time. The system not only achieves greater results than it could before, it also sustains those results as a new basis for functioning. The system literally evolves a different level of capability to be healthy and successful.

Sustaining new habits or results can seem a lot like climbing to a 14,000-foot mountain summit! The climb is rarely straight up; it crosses steep slopes and valleys to reach the top. Healthy systems sustain changes in much the same way. The cycle of a system which is learning how to sustain something new (like a different skill or attitude) shows phases of expansion, delays and sometimes, even downturns. Striking an appropriate balance of growth and stability, instead of just growth alone, helps the system incorporate changes it can count on for its future success.

Renewal

M.E. root, *renewen*, "to start over or become new again"

Definition: How a living system rejuvenates and heals

*A healthy living system restores its vital nature
and contributes to the vitality of others.*

Healthy living systems seek replenishment. They refuel by consuming nutrients, like water and food, and getting rid of wastes. These systems also rest. Rather than treating fallow periods as a squander of time, healthy systems find a sound balance between activity, where they expend energy, and Renewal, where they refill it. Renewal is the power every system has to regenerate, the investment it makes to re-establish Integrity. This investment makes the system healthier and more productive in its relationships, as well as more able to handle change.

Renewal is part of a natural cycle of living. As sung by the 60's band, The Byrds, and referenced in Ecclesiastes, there's a time to be born, a time to die, a time to plant, a time to reap, and a time for every purpose under heaven.[9,10] Stillness, rest and rejuvenation are just as important to optimal performance of a living system as staying active is.

The Essential Relationships

While the essentials are interesting as discrete principles, they are much more valuable when put into systematic practice. In actual use, they provide a holistic approach to success that's more apt to endure. *The 7 Essentials*sm is an organizing structure that stretches and directs the thinking and decisions of 21st century leaders to benefit the projects they lead.

Rather than a group of isolated elements, *The 7 Essentials*sm is an integrated framework, complete with inherent links between the essentials. It suggests that true power and sustainable wellth comes

True power and sustainable wellth comes through the union of opposites.

through the union of opposites—*active* with *receptive*, *masculine* with *feminine*, *willpower* with *acceptance*, *persevering* with *letting go*, a *pointed focus* with a *concern for the whole*, and ultimately, *becoming* with *being*. The dynamic interplay between these opposites is the natural pulsation of life.

Like a fractal of a hologram, each essential is one facet of an underlying goal: to generate healthy, sustainable results that respect the Integrity of the whole. The placement of each essential in the diagram above is purposeful, representing the inherent pulls and tensions that are part of closing the gap from where you are now to where you want to go and *to do so in a life-enhancing manner.*

For instance, when you apply *The 7 Essentials*[sm] to a professional challenge, three obvious tensions are:

- *Aspiration opposite of Sustainability*—Aspiration asks you to clarify your goals, while Sustainability means considering how you'll maintain your goals as a new way of operating. Aspiration draws you to a healthier, more compelling image of success; Sustainability makes sure that image of success becomes your reality. Working with these two essentials helps an inspired commitment last over time.

- *Innovation opposite of Simplicity*—Innovation invites you to take risks, experiment and learn from your experiences, like inventing an original idea or a fresh approach to a problem. Simplicity, on the other hand, calls you to stay alert to possibilities and focus on the path of ease. With these seemingly opposing essentials, you try out news ideas, pay attention to insights that emerge and actively choose the alternatives that lead to your desired results with less effort.

- *Movement opposite of Renewal*—Movement asks you to extend yourself through mindful, collaborative action. Renewal calls you to cultivate your energy within so that you are continually rejuvenated, resilient and ready for anything. Awareness of these two essentials enables you to respect the ebb and flow of achieving your goals.

Like a fractal of a hologram, each essential is one facet of an underlying goal: to generate healthy, sustainable results that respect the Integrity of the whole.

These are just three of the linkages in *The 7 Essentials*[sm] Perhaps the most significant relationship is the one every essential has to the center, Integrity.

While the other six essentials are important on their own, Integrity is what makes this framework quite unlike any other results-based change model.

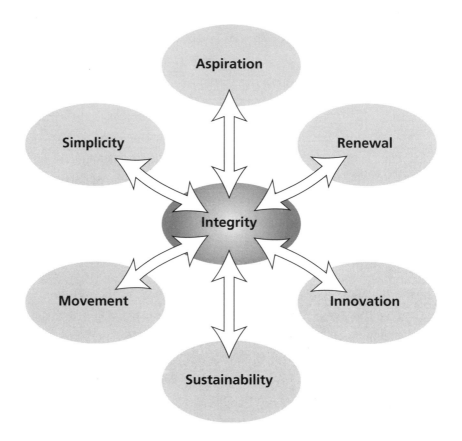

Integrity challenges you to think and act in ways that continually elevate the well-being of yourself and all those you interact with because *this is the best strategy for generating effective results now and over the long haul.* It is about affirming and evolving how you or any system you lead *already knows how to be competent, healthy and successful.* As a result, Integrity is the starting point, the lens that colors the questions and activities stimulated by the rest of the essentials. Integrity is what makes this framework truly wellth-generating rather than just another tool for managing or trying to control the dynamic situations you're in.

A Whole New Way of Achieving Results

The 7 Essentials^{sm} framework offers a whole new way of achieving results. Is it everything you need to know as a 21st century leader? No. You need considerable skills in managing finances, working with a diversity of ideas and people, collaborating with institutions that are quite unlike business and so on. However, this framework can help you organize your thoughts and decisions, no matter what your area of responsibility. It represents seven integrated capabilities that are foundational for enlightened success.

> **"The quality of our lives could be stunningly different if we based economic decisions on life values rather than purely financial values—a natural choice when owners live with the non-financial consequences of their decisions."** [11]
>
> **David Korten, author**

The framework advocates that you appreciate the brilliance of every healthy living system to self-organize, self-determine, self-regulate and self-regenerate. The model also helps you explore how the quality of your questions and decisions might be different if you based them first and foremost on advancing life.

The central purpose of this leadership tool is *to create wellth, a healthier form of results that is naturally sustainable because it appreciates the whole of life and its inherent processes.* Within this context, the tool offers a variety of specific applications for 21st century leaders.

The following two applications of *The 7 Essentials*^{sm} are outlined in Chapters 5 and 6. We recommend that you experiment with these applications before using the tool in any other way:

- *Making It Personal*—The central ingredient of healthy results and the systems that create them is Integrity. The same goes for leaders and organizations who want to lead at their sustainable best. For that reason, the most valuable application is to apply Integrity to you as a leader. Chapter 6 provides tools and exercises so that you maximize your core purpose, values and strengths in whatever you do and lead with greater excellence and ease. Read and apply the exercises in this chapter before you do anything else.

- *Asking Better Questions*—Most leaders don't realize that their questions automatically skew their decisions and answers. Ironically, effectively diagnosing a challenge you face demands strategic questions that open up thinking rather than shut thinking down. Plus, by asking strategic questions, you're more able to coach yourself and others to convert seeming breakdowns into breakthroughs in personal life, business and society. Chapter 7 helps you use *The 7 Essentials*^{sm} to do just that.

The 7 Essentials^{sm}—Test It for Yourself

The 7 Essentials^{sm} has these characteristics:

- **It's scale-able.** That is, *The 7 Essentials*^{sm} can be used at multiple levels, from your personal life to your business success to your social contributions.

- **It's derived from theory and experience** rather than theory alone.

- **It's a truth, not The Truth.** It is a mental model that is always revisable and updateable, especially as our collective human knowledge expands.

- **It's a tool for systemic thinking and action.** The tool is not the answer itself, but aids you in finding new answers for yourself.

- **It's a set of core patterns** found across disciplines, old and new, that can help you create healthy forms of success in modern times.

- **It's centered in Integrity,** encouraging you to discover the way you, or any system of your concern, knows how to be healthy, effective and successful by design.

- **It's a technology for shifting to 21st century leadership**, the kind of leadership that's driven to cultivate total health and effectiveness.

But don't take our word for it. Diligently use this framework for a concerted period of time, and notice the effects. Approach it with your intellect and your heart, and pay attention to what arises in your experience. Look for evidence that tells you this framework is or isn't for you.

For instance, does it help you ask questions that you don't usually ask? Are you clearer about the outcomes you want and what you'll do to sustain them? Are you able to consciously make better decisions than before? Do you see new opportunities in the complexities you face? Do you experience a different quality of wellness and effectiveness in your life and your leadership? Are you better equipped to support others in generating new capabilities and results? Does the framework move you in a direction of being a wiser leader? Notice where the framework aligns with your experience and where it stretches you to think from a totally different frame of reference.

The Charge of the 21st Century Leader

The 7 Essentials^{sm} poses a challenge for you as a 21st century leader: to amplify and widen your abilities to achieve and sustain healthy results for yourself, your organization and beyond. This 21st century leadership charge also includes building the capabilities within people and whole systems to generate greater health and effectiveness for themselves.

> *The 7 Essentials*^{sm} poses a challenge for you as a 21st century leader: to amplify and widen your abilities to achieve and sustain healthy results for yourself, your organization and beyond.

Your role as a 21st century leader is pivotal. It is in this role where you utilize your presence and talents to create a healthier life for yourself and your company, plus pave the way for others to do the same. Through deep study and practice of *The 7 Essentials*,^{sm} you develop lifelong skills to consistently attain results with greater wisdom no matter what situation you're in. We believe *The 7 Essentials*^{sm} is a bridge to help you lead from a life-centric approach and to fully step up to the role of 21st century leadership with greater power, progress and wellth.

Chapter Highlights

- The 7 Essentials^{sm} *is an integral leadership framework that helps you holistically consider the complex problems you face. It equips you to operate from a wellth-driven approach to success.*

- The 7 Essentials^{sm} *helps you answer the question:* Given the challenge I'm facing, how can I achieve and sustain success in a healthy, life-enhancing way?

- The 7 Essentials^{sm} *includes seven capabilities that are instrumental for realizing constructive results: Integrity, Aspiration, Innovation, Movement, Simplicity, Sustainability and Renewal.*

- The 7 Essentials^{sm} *is a whole new way of achieving results, particularly suited for ill-structured problems, such as challenges that are unpredictable, complex and unclear. These are challenges without clear-cut paths laid out for you; you must make it up as you go along. These issues require a whole new approach so you transcend them rather than deal with the same problem over again.*

- *21st century leadership is the pivotal role that generates significance along with success.* The 7 Essentials^{sm} *enables you to fully step up to the role of 21st century leadership with greater power, progress and wellth.*

making it personal

—

"Modern technology is creating a society of such complex diversity and richness that most people have a greater range of personal choice, wider experience and a more highly developed sense of self-worth than ever before. For the first time, the common man has the opportunity to establish his own identity, to determine who he will be."[1]

R. Buckminster Fuller, American inventor, architect,
engineer, mathematician, poet and cosmologist

"To think, to hope and to dream are abilities enjoyed by people throughout the world, regardless of culture, gender, race or social status. In improving ourselves—and thus the world—the first step is to recognize the unbreakable links between our inner world of ideas, thoughts and concepts and the external world of event and circumstance. Just because our world today is so changeable and volatile is no reason for despair. Quite the contrary, for the reason why we now live in a world that is changing more rapidly than at any time before in human history, is precisely because individuals have unprecedented power. … Everything depends on our power of choice."[2]

from the Peace Messenger Initiative dedicated to the United Nations

---

making it personal

how you can lead with Integrity
(and why to do so right now)

As you've already seen, *The 7 Essentials*[sm] framework revolves around Integrity, an essential that is more than simply good ethics. Integrity is the primary resource that personalizes, re-energizes and strengthens your leadership.

When you lead with Integrity, you experience well-being and better performance. You operate from genuine *values* and bring superior *value* to everything you accomplish. Your organization learns how to design and manage its activities from an impetus that's more encompassing than the maximization of profits. Integrity gives the organization an unwavering sense of purpose which stands behind everything it does. In effect, Integrity enhances 21st century leadership on all fronts.

> **Integrity is the primary resource that personalizes, re-energizes and strengthens your leadership.**

Leading with Integrity has become imperative in the last decade. As countless businesses have gone from feast to famine, the strains on leadership have been fierce. Many leaders are even accused of suffering a hangover from the economic binge their companies used to enjoy.[3] Yet, unrestrained profit-making strategies clearly haven't created organizations or leaders of resilience. Plus, the success-at-any-cost leadership style is not without consequences: consumer confidence in leaders today is lower than ever before, numerous businesses have eroded their very foundations of success and, leaders frequently leave the office each day feeling hollow, ineffective and spent.

As a 21st century business leader, this puts you under a lot of pressure.

You must increase profits in the midst of a turbulent economy yet, at the same time, create a company that is about something that outlasts profit, something that keeps people motivated even if profit declines. More than that, you must find a way to make balanced and sane judgments even when surrounded by distractions that tempt you to overreact.

John Knapp, Director of the Southern Institute for Business and Professional Ethics, claims that the economic boon of the 1990s taught a whole generation of corporate leaders "to focus on short-term profitability instead of considering what's best for a company in the long run",[4] not to mention what's best for society. Sadly, both businesses and society pay the penalties today for careless business strategies applied only a decade ago.

Leading from Integrity is the key. But, you can't do that by just reading a book; you have to *make Integrity personal.*

Gaining New Life from Integrity

When Barbara was passed over for a big promotion, she was distraught. More than distraught, she was plainly beside herself. Having spent most of her adult career upwardly mobile in a high-tech firm, Barbara wasn't sure who she was apart from her job. Her friends were company employees, her energies concentrated on work, and her title as marketing director a hard-won part of her identity. So, when she wasn't even considered for a job she assumed she was next in line for, she fell flatly into an identity crisis. Her world turned upside-down.

We can relate to Barbara's situation. Even the most enlightened of us identify with our titles (like 'mother,' 'coach' or 'director'), our span of authority or what we own. Our sense of security often comes from what's outside us instead of from what's within.

However, all of a sudden, everything can shift. We are fired from a job with no forewarning, the stock market dives and we wind up in mounds of debt, we get pregnant when a baby isn't part of our plans, our country goes to war. The world changes constantly, and we don't have much control over it. Without the inner anchor of Integrity to help us stay poised and productive, everything can go haywire. We can be thrown off center.

Integrity breathes new life into leadership effectiveness. It is an inner source of power to deal with the outer complexities of life. It's the quality of wholeness and completeness[5] of every living system, broader than just ethics. Not that ethics aren't important; ethics are crucial, no longer optional in the game of business. In fact, the activities of leaders and corporations are more transparent than ever before, and good ethics are the *price of entry* to entertain doing business at all.

Integrity is how you, or any system, are naturally healthiest, most successful and whole.

Nevertheless, as discussed in Chapter 5, Integrity goes well beyond ethical behavior. In *The 7 Essentials*,[sm] Integrity is how you, or any system, are naturally healthiest, most successful and whole.

Living systems function best when they work in accordance with their whole nature, respecting how they're *already designed* to be healthy. From this perspective, *whole, ecological, authentic, capable* and *well* join the concepts *ethical* and *conscientious* to convey the robustness of what Integrity means.

What Integrity Means
for 21st Century Leaders

Leading from Integrity is about leading with a sense of wholeness and effectiveness, where you naturally work at your optimum. In contrast, a lack of Integrity is when something isn't whole, not working at its best, like when a mirror cracks and a few shards fall out. Perhaps some aspect of your self is cut off or disenfranchised, disabled from helping you lead. Perhaps you've forgotten the deeper reasons why you're leading in the first place. Maybe you're ignoring your own standards of success or disregarding what you're actually good at. When you fail to lead with Integrity, your leadership is compromised. The same thing can happen to your company.

"The process of becoming a leader is much the same as becoming an integrated human being." [6]

Warren Bennis, author

As a 21st century leader, one way to transform stress into greater success is to promote Integrity in action wherever you are. This means helping yourself and others reconnect with an innate wisdom for being healthy, whole and successful. Instead of settling for mediocrity or knee-jerk reactions, your task is to foster the kind of relationship that optimizes wellth in all you do, and this begins with Integrity. Yet, operating from Integrity may require different strategies than you're accustomed to.

For starters, *who you are* is a big part of the equation. Your personal Integrity affects your ability to attain healthier results, whether in your life, your family or your business. Consequently, as a 21st century leader, the first and foremost strategy for achieving and sustaining healthy results begins with how you bring the best of yourself into life and work. (To better understand how to use your health as a positive resource for leading, take the *Personal Wellth Quotient* assessment in Chapter 3.)

> As a 21st century leader, the first and foremost strategy for achieving and sustaining healthy results begins with how you bring the best of yourself into life and work.

The promise of living and leading from Integrity is that it will help you *thrive* regardless of the conditions you face. You'll be better equipped to cope with an increasing amount of change, learn from it and evolve new insights and capabilities as a result. You'll be more resilient, and even when your world seems on its head, able to shape a brighter future. Because of your deep, abiding sense of Integrity, an inner foundation will set the tone for who you are and everything you do.

Out of Integrity?
The Warning Signs

How do you know if you should re-center your leadership with Integrity? Here are a few warning signs that tell you it's time to make adjustments:

☑ *You have a hard time assimilating new information, innovating with new ideas or learning.* It seems like life is coming at you too fast, and most of the time you feel overloaded and overwhelmed. You don't seem to have clear boundaries for making discerning decisions in the middle of this chaos.

☑ *You are unable to sustain results* in a way that's healthy for you.

☑ *You are less efficient and productive than you'd expect.* Plus, you don't know exactly how to bring your strengths to bear in your role.

☑ *You are living and leading in conflict* with your personal values.

☑ *Your sense of success is completely tied up in attaining money, prestige or responsibilities*, often at the expense of a deeper quality of happiness.

☑ *You want to return passion to your leadership*, instead of just going through the motions.

☑ *You are in the habit of depersonalizing and objectifying others.* This can be to such an extent that you feel like relationships are a nuisance rather than core to your success. As a result, you may even find yourself in breakdowns with employees, family members, colleagues and clients.

☑ *You have an inescapable feeling of personal inadequacy and emptiness.* Your accomplishments don't mean as much as they once did. Even if you've stayed highly involved in your leadership role, you've lost contact with the bigger reasons behind it.

☑ *You hear distress in your voice*: My work feels arduous. I'm tired all the time. Why do I do this every day? I can't seem to strike a healthy balance in my life and work. I have nothing left to give.

☑ *You suffer physical and emotional symptoms*, like chronic tension, nagging colds, depression, heart ailments, cancer and other lifestyle maladies. To make matters worse, your gut tells you these are tied to how you're living and working.

If you experience any of these warning signs, you are *already* compromising your success as a leader, both in life and work. You aren't paying attention to what it takes for you to be whole and effective, nor are you using your health as a resource for powerful leadership. Surprisingly, many of us live with these signs for so long that we believe they're the norm. We think these signals are the price to pay for taking on the stance of leadership rather than symptoms trying to tell us to realign our lives with a new definition of freedom, balanced success and wellth.

The Elements of Integrity

Leading with Integrity is about affirming the deeper inner truths that produce wellth in outer life. It's about shaping your decisions from these truths rather than allowing the world to choose for you. It's about having a healthier relationship with yourself so that you have healthier relationships with others. It's about a *personalized model of leadership*, your individual theory-in-action regarding what creates healthy and sustained success.

> Integrity is about a personalized model of leadership, where you affirm deeper inner truths that produce wellth in your outer life and work.

As a 21st century leader, three elements are crucial for operating with Integrity: core purpose, enduring values and natural strengths.

1 **Core purpose**—Core purpose is your answer to the question, *Why do I exist?* It's why you choose to lead. Your core purpose provides a firm foundation to your work, the ground of everything you do and the legacy you intend to leave. It is your deeper leadership directive.

2 **Enduring values**—Enduring values are your response to the question, *What do I truly stand for?* These are the principles, ideals and ethics that guide your thinking and actions, the standards of success that you find compelling and worthwhile.

3 **Natural strengths**—Answering *What do I excel at?* identifies your natural strengths. Strengths are your "near perfect performance in an activity,"[7] those talents that enable you to actualize your purpose as well as surpass the results of others.

Your strengths are what you do effortlessly, what you seem to be meant to do.

Purpose, values and strengths are the central, wellth-oriented tools for enlightened 21st century leadership. They're the heart and soul of how and why you lead, your intangible leadership assets. Together, they bring a sense of meaning and aliveness to your life and work. By continually realigning your thoughts and actions to these elements, you maintain leadership Integrity, which is your ability to generate and regenerate good health and performance. Plus, these three elements serve as an organizing force that attracts the right people, projects and prospects to you.

> Integrity gives you an inexhaustible resource and an inner authority from which to lead. It's a principal strategy for improving your leadership performance, especially in a world filled with complex problems around every bend.

Realize that your purpose, values and strengths won't tell you how you lead. Instead, these elements help you know what choices are healthy for you and what choices aren't. They provide internally-defined boundaries for life-enhancing leadership decisions. At the same time these elements *accelerate* your success, they also provide you a healthy way to *moderate* it.

When your leadership is solidly founded in these attributes, you're less likely to drift away from your peak. You're more likely to find leadership opportunities that enhance your life and your business at the same time. Plus, you cultivate a fortitude within that cannot be taken away. Integrity gives you an inexhaustible resource and an inner authority from which to lead. It's a principal strategy for improving your leadership performance, especially in a world filled with complex problems around every bend. Your responsibility as a 21st century leader is to learn how to operate with Integrity regardless of the challenge before you and to help other systems do the same.

Integrity by Design: Making it Work for You

1. Discovering Your Core Purpose

As head of the global company's communication department, Dianne, one of our executive clients, faced budget cuts for the third time in a year. So, she couldn't hire the additional staff she needed to get work done. But the demands on her didn't diminish. In fact, she was constantly asked to do more with less, a minute-by-minute juggle between producing internal employee updates, managing public relations and making sure Wall Street was informed about the company's fiscal outlook.

> "Your work is to discover your work, and then with all your heart to give yourself to it."[8]
>
> Gautama Buddha

Her role was indispensable in order to keep the public and the workforce upbeat about the company, yet she wasn't playing the role she originally signed up for. She hired on to lead the company's communication efforts more strategically, to get ahead of the curve, not wear the hats of writer, producer, project manager and, most of all, *chief reactor*. Regardless, here she was, contractually committed for the next three years and amazingly less prone to the impulsiveness her crazy-making circumstances seemed to warrant.

> "A life of purpose is the purpose of life."[9]
>
> Deepak Chopra, physician and author

Ask Dianne how she's thriving when other company leaders are barely surviving and she'll say it's because of her *core purpose*. In a time when any other leader might have left the company or resented the never-ending demands, Dianne uses the turmoil as a chance to doggedly rediscover the deeper reasons she became a leader in the first place. Her conclusion?

- To build a positive future for the company.

- To continually provide clarity and direction for her department, and protect that focus from being eroded.

- To help people open new doors of possibilities that they never believed were available to them before.

Simple statements, yet powerful in how they affect her attitude, her relationships with clients and her department's results.

Discovering her core purpose wasn't just an irrelevant exercise. Dianne applies her purpose everyday to guide her thinking, make decisions and re-focus her attention on what's important when she gets off track. More importantly, Dianne's core purpose keeps her connected to her motives for leading. Frequently, this is her saving grace. Having a clear purpose stops her from getting caught in the reactive snare that traps so many of her peers.

Dianne wakes up knowing what path she's on and why she chose it; this keeps her leadership alive. Not surprisingly, her passion is noticed by others. Clients, vendors and employees want to work around her because she exudes something optimistic and vibrant.

> "Purpose is spirit seeking expression. It converts average organizations into exceptional ones; it transforms employees into co-partners; it creates leaders out of managers."[10]
>
> Kevin Cashman, LeaderSource

All living systems, including you, have a reason for being, or a purpose to fulfill. Your purpose isn't a job title, and it isn't something you have to create out of thin air. Nor is it something you find out there somewhere. Author David Hutchens says, "Rather, it is something you discover as you pay attention to where your life is most fulfilling, and where you find the most joy and meaning. Your task is to seek deeper awareness of your purpose as it unfolds over time."[11]

Your purpose "is something you discover as you pay attention to where your life is most fulfilling, and where you find the most joy and meaning. Your task is to seek deeper awareness of your purpose as it unfolds over time."[12]

Discovering your purpose starts by asking: *Why do I exist?* This is a soulful question, and when you engage in it earnestly, it provides you with a depth of insight that will remain fairly stable in life, no matter what role or situation you are in. For example, here are a few of the sincere purpose statements of individual leaders we've coached:

- To communicate authenticity and truth.

- To maximize the best in people and situations.

- To integrate Eastern and Western ideas into a new paradigm for living, working and managing business.

- To bridge the cultural, financial and digital divides with global technologies.

Knowing your core purpose is a level of self awareness that allows you to live and lead *purpose-fully*.

21st Century Leadership in Action:
Discovering Your Core Purpose

Take a few moments to consider the deeper purpose or purposes that drive your life. (If possible, reflect on this over a period of time, instead of just one sitting.) Remember that your core purpose:

- *Captures your fundamental reason for existence*

- *Has meaning to you personally, regardless of what others think*

- *Guides and inspires how you live*

- *Is tight enough to help you set healthy boundaries, yet large enough that you have room to grow into it*

- *Is a thread that runs through your life (meaning, you will likely notice how it has shaped the decisions you've made in the past)*

- *Is timeless*

- *May feel like a profound or sacred connection*

- *Reflects you at your healthiest and most fulfilled*

- *Answers the question,* Why do I exist?

Write your purpose(s) on a piece of paper. Don't worry about creating a single purpose statement that says it all. The goal is to have a fuller and embodied sense of your purpose and to calibrate your decisions based on it so that you deliver healthy, sustainable results.

Once you have a sense of your core purpose, consider the kind of leader your purpose calls you to be. What qualities of leadership would you put into effect if you were leading from your core purpose every day? What would it take to lead with those qualities right now?

2. Living Your Enduring Values

Mark felt like a fish out of water. His CEO demanded that he hard-sell the company's newest and most pricey computers, but the more Mark goaded customers to buy, the lower his actual sales fell. It wasn't that he couldn't close a deal, he just felt uneasy doing something against his principles. He preferred to educate customers about the full range of technical products and let them choose what worked for them rather than sell them features they didn't need. But, he knew he wasn't going to change the values of the company. Instead, he found a sales job at a different computer manufacturer, this time one aligned with his inner standards.

> "Always be a first-rate version of yourself, instead of a second-rate version of somebody else."[13]
>
> Judy Garland, actress and singer

Mark holds *informed choice* high in his chain of values. He believes that consumers are generally smart and can make good decisions once they understand the pros and cons. Like Mark, all of us serve some sort of value system whether we know it or not, a set of beliefs that undergird how we think and behave. Bill O'Brien, former CEO of Hanover Insurance, says that values are "deeply held convictions that have a profound effect on the direction of our lives. [Values] serve as central organizing principles that help us decide how to address complex situations and problems as they bombard us."[14] Like wearing a pair of glasses, our values are the lens through which we observe and judge the activities of life. There is no time when our values don't color what we see and do.

Values are "deeply held convictions that have a profound effect on the direction of our lives. [Values] serve as central organizing principles that help us decide how to address complex situations and problems as they bombard us."[15]

21st century leaders get in touch with the values by which they want to live and lead, replacing inferior or antiquated beliefs with value systems that address the higher order needs of people, nature and societies. As described in Chapters 1 and 2, these leaders lean toward values that are life-centric, such as right action, compassion, human dignity, self-reliance, collaboration, accountability, excellence, inclusiveness and, most of all, total health. Plus, they enable every individual and every culture to adopt and adapt values that work for them as long as those values do no harm to others. Closer to home, 21st century leaders challenge themselves to become better people by consistently putting their values into practice.

> **"If you really push people, they'll agree that virtue is more important than money."** [16]
>
> Martha Nussbaum, leading philosopher

21st Century Leadership in Action:
Living Your Enduring Values

List three to five values that challenge you to continually become a better person, and explore why these particular values are important to you. Remember, values:

- *Are special and unique to you*

- *Are the logic or motivation behind your actions*

- *Provide boundaries for what you tolerate and what you don't*

- *Last over a period of time*

- *Motivate you to rise to a new quality of living and leading*

- *Evolve and deepen as you gain new experiences and awarenesses*

- *Answer the question:* What do I truly stand for?

How will you use these values in your leadership today? How will your values equip you to create healthier results, manage the growth of your company or team, make decisions and lead others? How will you stop using old, worn out values that no longer work well?

3. Exercising Your Natural Strengths

Miguel had a knack for sincerity and directness. He felt no discomfort in sharing his opinions candidly, even if that meant opposing his peers. He believed that it was necessary to be outspoken and to openly deal with difficult circumstances in order to resolve them, no matter how ugly or awkward it felt. For him, avoiding a problem only caused a delay in what could be positive movement toward a solution. *Confrontation* was Mark's natural-born strength.

21st century leaders use their natural-born strengths as a means to excel. They get up every morning and do what comes easily to them: *exercise their strengths and manage around their weaknesses.* The act of leading from their strengths gives them a sense of pleasure and gratification, and it's an antidote to the burnout and frustrations most other leaders face. Of course, many situations require 21st century leaders to learn new knowledge or improve certain skills, but their strengths direct their leadership style. Leading this way takes less effort because strengths are an inherent source of self-mastery.

Like Miguel, we all have strengths intrinsic to operating at our best. The latest strength-based research says that throughout life, the seeds of strengths are hidden in what you yearn for (what unfailingly draws your attention), what you seem to learn more rapidly than others, how you spontaneously react and what satisfies you most.[17] You only have to legitimize and proactively apply your strengths to lead with greater ease, effectiveness and wellth.

Your strengths are hidden in what you yearn for (what unfailingly draws your attention), what you seem to learn more rapidly than others, how you spontaneously react to situations before thinking about it and what satisfies you most.[18]

Emphasizing strengths is quite a switch from doctrines that teach managers to look for flaws and deficits. Most leaders learn this conventional philosophy at one time or another. It advises leaders to develop their weaknesses in order to become well-rounded rather than to capitalize on what they already do innately well. Well-roundedness isn't a bad goal by itself. But it isn't the world-class performance to which the majority of leaders and companies aspire.

Plus, the consequences of this flaw-based approach can be costly. Leaders that subscribe to it are likely to have organizational training programs, designs and processes that incrementally refine people's skills rather than maximize people's talents.[19] In essence, they design their management styles and organizations for mediocrity.

Gallup, the well-known opinion polling organization, recently completed a comprehensive study of excellence. After investigating more than "1.7 million employees in 101 companies from 63 countries," Gallup found that "only 20 percent actually feel their strengths are at play every day." Alarmingly, this number decreases as the employee moves up the ladder. No surprise, however, that employees who utilize their strengths were "50 percent more likely to work in business units with lower employee turnover, 38 percent more likely to work in more productive business units, and 44 percent more likely to work in business units with higher customer satisfaction scores."[20]

21st Century Leadership in Action:
Exercising Your Natural Strengths

Reflect on the three to five of your innate strengths, those ways of thinking and acting in which you seem to excel regardless of the situation. Remember, your strengths are:

- *What you do consistently and with near perfection*

- *Activities where you experience a sense of flow, effortlessness and mastery*

- *Yearnings, rapid learnings, spontaneous top-of-mind reactions and deeper satisfactions*

- *How your mind and body are already designed and inclined to work*

- *Proven gifts you've shown over the course of your lifetime*

- *What you can imagine doing repeatedly, happily and successfully*

- *Your answer to the question,* At what do I naturally excel?

Now consider how to capitalize on your strengths within your leadership. What shifts do you need to make so that you lead with your true strengths, instead of leading with what you assume other people assess your strengths to be?

Making Integrity Work for Your Organization

Clear purpose, values and strengths are undoubtedly tools for personal leadership. They establish healthy boundaries to channel your energy and actions, and they help you know when to say *yes* and when to say *no* to choices that come your way. Keep these tools in the forefront of your mind everyday. They're your foundation for individual, wellth-driven success.

In addition, these tools of Integrity work for your organization. Remember, *The 7 Essentials*^{sm} is a scale-able framework. The same principle of Integrity applies to your business just as it does to your leadership and your life.

> "Leadership is lifting a person's vision to higher sights, the raising of a person's performance to a higher standard, the building of a personality beyond its normal limitations." [21]
>
> Peter Drucker, management expert

Like 21st century leaders, 21st century companies conduct business from a core of Integrity by conscious design. They structure everything they do around that core. And, like 21st century leaders, these companies ask the harder, yet central, wellth-directed questions of Integrity that other companies fail to consider:

What is our core purpose?

What deeper values will consistently guide our decisions and actions?

What are our natural strengths? How will we take advantage of our strengths in order to excel?

Plus, 21st century companies extend these questions even further:

How will we use our purpose, values and strengths to manage the growth of our business?

How will our purpose, values
and strengths shape:
the identity of our company?
our brands?
how we develop and supply our
products and services?
how we communicate, whether
in-house or publicly?

How will we respect the purpose, values
and strengths of other organizations and
societies so that, through our relationship,
we foster mutual wellth?

Companies that commit to Integrity find that their core purpose, values and innate strengths permeate their corporate culture, leaving no business activity untouched. This includes *everything*, from how they use the talents of their workforce and care for customers to how they design and sell their products and function within society. 21st century companies know that *Integrity is the core structure for advancing sustainable progress.*

"There is a growing legion of business people who are hungry to build something of enduring character on a set of values they can be proud of." [22]

Jim Collins, author and management researcher

As examples, you may recognize the deep-rooted purpose, values and strengths of these 21st century organizations: [23, 24, 25]

Organization	Their Purpose	A Few of their Values	A Few of their Strengths
Whistler Ski Resort	To be the premier mountain resort community.	A strong, healthy community—where growth and development are managed and controlled, where the needs of residents are met, where community life and individual well-being are fostered, where the diversity of people is celebrated, and where social interactions, recreation, culture, health services and lifelong learning are accessible to all. Protecting our natural environment and our role as responsible guardians of it, respecting and preserving nature's wealth for present and future generations. Sound fiscal management to sustain a healthy economy through thoughtful, long-range financial planning.	Creating powerful, win-win partnerships with organizations and the surrounding community Environmental management Top-notch recreational opportunities
Freeplay Energy Group	To provide access to energy to everybody all the time.	Results orientated—Delivering on promises to shareholders and partners. Leading-edge—On the edge of technology and business practice. Responsible—Being responsible towards our employees, the environment and the communities we touch. A friend and partner—Taking a positive attitude to developing partnerships and friendships based on trust.	Research and development of renewable technologies, such as wind-up radios and flashlights
Merck & Company	To preserve and improve human and animal life.	We are committed to the highest standards of ethics and integrity. We expect profits, but only from work that satisfies customer needs and benefits humanity.	Scientific acumen and partnerships to produce high quality medicines and spread them to places around the world

Competitors can imitate your organization's structure, market strategies and business practices. But, the structures of Integrity are part of what makes your company distinct. No other business can replicate your Integrity, even when they try.

Stonyfield Farms is living proof. When Groupe Danone, a leader in the food industry, with such brands as Dannon and Evian plus over 100,000 employees in 120 countries, first attempted to enter the U.S. natural foods market with a new organic-style yogurt, they failed. Unlike the market leader, Stonyfield Farms, an $80 million company dedicated to the values of personal health and environmental sustainability, Groupe Danone wasn't known for a commitment to social responsibility that wellness-driven consumers desired. Groupe Danone had immense resources to create a good product and deliver it to a widespread market (maybe even more efficiently than Stonyfield), but they couldn't recreate the Stonyfield essence that drew consumers to buy the product.

68 percent of consumers are willing to pay higher prices for products and services from organizations that stand for enduring purpose and principles.[26]

CEO and President of Stonyfield, Gary Hirshberg, explains that eventually Groupe Danone chose another route to capture the organic foods market: they financially invested in Stonyfield, acquiring 40 percent ownership in the company yet also protecting the Stonyfield values and strengths (Stonyfield's intangible assets) that consumers found so appealing. Both companies win. Groupe Danone gains the market access it desires while Stonyfield retains the style of responsible leadership for which it's known.[27]

Managing Integrity-centered organizations is a strategic way that 21st century leaders use business to propagate a global culture of health and sustainability. Yet, more often than not, 21st century companies with this business ethos gain superb benefits they hadn't planned on:

- *The company finds their products and services uniquely differentiated in the marketplace* as competitors literally can't mimic the soul of their brands or their corporate identity. Most companies position their brands solely on customer appeal and must change this positioning with the shift of customers' whims. Integrity-centered companies draw on their core purpose, values and strengths as part of their reputation in order to powerfully promote their brands. Their unwavering dedication to Integrity is a difference consumers can count on.

- *The company discovers that consumers have a deep trust and respect for who they are,* a loyalty that sticks through thick and thin. (See *A Tale of Resilience* to find out how the Integrity of one company paid off when the economy went sour.)

A Tale of Resilience

For companies who lead with Integrity, growth frequently occurs not only in the boon times but also in a soft economy. Although most of 2001-2002 was a period of loss and layoffs for most companies in the supermarket industry, North American grocer, Whole Foods, attributes its *increases* in revenue to the 25 percent of customers who did 75 percent of the chain's business. These customers felt a bond between their personal values and the mission, values and trustworthy brands of this grocery store. This allegiance buoyed Whole Foods' financial performance even when economic pressures were intense.[28]

- *The company enjoys an easier flow in getting work done* as each part of the organization connects through shared purpose, values and an appreciation of their respective strengths, and builds synergies off the other.

- *The company makes better hiring decisions.* With a distinctive purpose, values and strengths in their organizations and teams, leaders are better able to hire employees that are a good fit, as well as those who will be able to stretch the organization in innovative and positive directions.

- *The company benefits from streamlined marketing efforts.* Their promotional and advertising messages are crisp, clear and coherent because company communications, whether in a marketing campaign or a political campaign, stem from the same enduring principles and priorities.

- *The company has a stable, wellth-driven culture and a focused, energized workforce.* Employees know who they are, what brands they sell, what customers they serve and how they distinctively serve these customers best. Ironically, since the company's fundamentals are reliable and clear, employees don't need to question these in every decision. Employees' energies are freed to explore innovative ways of doing business, with Integrity as their footing.

- *The company makes quicker and more mindful decisions.* Leaders and employees can more skillfully choose courses of action due to the *internal criteria for success* woven into the company's character. Their purposes, values and inherent strengths provide them a *backboard* to instinctively (and often, courageously) bounce ideas, challenges and concerns against. And, this gives them a sense of *backbone* in the eyes of their stakeholders.

Consider case in point: Tom's of Maine, a company located in quaint Kennebunk, Maine, and led by CEO Tom Chappell. Tom's of Maine supplies products for oral, body and wellness care. With record-breaking gross sales that exceeded $35 million in 2001 and over 30 years of experience under its belt, Tom's knows what it means to be fiscally prosperous in its industry.

Yet, making money is far from the sole aim of this company. Tom's *core purpose* is actually fourfold:[31]

1 Serve customer's health needs with imaginative science from plants and minerals.

2 Inspire all those they serve with a mission of responsibility and goodness.

3 Empower others by sharing their knowledge, time, talents and profits.

4 Help create a better world by exchanging with others their faith, experience and hope.

Likewise, Tom's ask its leaders to make strategic and tactical decisions with four values equally in mind: *financial profit, customer joy, societal good and environmental health.* Chappell contends that Tom's success continues to be built everyday as workers incorporate their core purpose and values into the company's very operating system.

Take, for instance, the way Tom's purpose and values inspire how they develop, manufacture and sell products. Tom's makes clear assurances to employees, investors and consumers that the company will:

- Produce products made of simple, high-quality and natural ingredients.

- Package products using containers that are not only recyclable and biodegradable, but also educational. This way consumers can make informed decisions about purchasing the product and responsibly disposing of it after consumption.

- Ensure products are sufficiently researched (without animal testing), compliant with regulatory standards, safe and effective.

- Value everyone engaged in the product's creation. This includes everyone, from respecting the basic human rights of indigenous cultures where natural ingredients are harvested to maximizing the genius of employees and suppliers so that they yield products of the highest caliber. This also means accounting for the well-being of present and future generations when making any product decisions today.

- Price products so that the company can afford to produce them and the customer feels good about buying them.

- Make product claims clear and honest to the consumer, the company, government agencies (such as the Food & Drug Administration) and other certifying organizations (such as the American Dental Association).

Yet, Tom's success goes beyond its purpose and values; the company also relies on its *natural strengths*, of which one is *education*. From the instructional insert found in the toothpaste box to the label on the bottle of decongestant cough syrup to Tom's community stewardship programs, the company teaches its consumer not only about the Integrity of Tom's brand, but also about the larger aims of the organization and the health of the world.

> **"In the next society, the biggest challenge for the large company—especially for the multinational—may be its social legitimacy: its values, it mission, its vision."** [33]
>
> Peter Drucker

Tom's knows that every connection with its consumer network is another moment the company can actualize its core purpose in a grander style. Managing with Integrity is the way Tom's of Maine dares to create a healthier world, challenge its consumers and employees to contribute their part and demonstrate financial profitability at the same time. [32]

Clearly, out of *The 7 Essentials*[sm] leadership framework, the essential of Integrity most calls you to create a wellth-driven economy, external and internal to your life and your business, so that you produce beneficial and sustainable forms of health and success.

21st Century Companies:
Benchmarks of Integrity

If you lead a 21st century company of Integrity, you probably notice...	If you lead a company without a clear sense of Integrity, you probably notice...
An interest in the long-lasting health of your organization by stakeholders as diverse as leaders, workers, customers, suppliers, distributors and society	Stakeholders that don't take a real interest in your long term health or they believe the company is only concerned with self-pursuits (usually defined by profit)
A clarity of purpose, strengths and values held by leaders, employees and, many times, your consumers	A lack of clear purpose, values, or recognizable strengths by your leaders, employees and consumers
Brands, aligned with the Integrity of your company, that allow you to create steadfast consumer bonds	Brand messages and company messages that send mixed signals to consumers, often resulting in consumer mistrust
Synergies between your departments, as well as all along your value-generating chain	Lack of collaboration in your value chain since no one really understands how they play a part in company performance overall
Consistent communications inside and outside your company	Public communications about your performance which appeals to Wall Street, yet internal realities that tell a different story
Company decisions driven by a genuine desire for business growth and profit, social good, customer delight and product excellence	Company decisions driven by the desire to increase financial results or to pursue unrestrained business growth
Healthy, energizing and manageable levels of stress in your work environment	Significant burnout of leaders and employees or a demoralized workforce
Networks of consumers, employees and devoted stakeholders naturally forming around your brand identity	No real personal connection between your consumers or employees and the identity of your brands or company
Employees and leaders who enjoy personal and professional growth just by affiliating with your company	Employees and leaders without the skills to do their jobs and often searching elsewhere for more meaningful work

Integrity: The Heart of Generating Wellth

It is no accident that Integrity is at the heart of *The 7 Essentials,*^{sm} our framework to assist 21st century leaders in generating new levels of wellth. The premise of Integrity—*to enable a system to naturally operate at its most healthy, whole and successful*—is the centerpiece from which the other essentials stem. After strengthening Integrity, each of the other essentials offers further avenues to apply to your self and your organization:

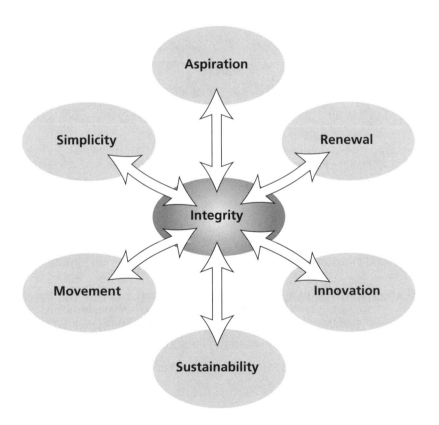

- *Integrity + Aspiration* radically expands your definition of success so that your results benefit you, your company, your workforce and the broader social, cultural and environmental contexts in which you work.

- *Integrity + Innovation* asks you to take risks and learn from leadership, product, organizational and business innovations that are aligned with your purpose, core values and strengths.

- *Integrity + Movement* prompts you to act in ways that are decisive, timely and ethical during the good times as well as the bad, the kind of *right action* you can be proud of without regret.

- *Integrity + Simplicity* helps you make streamlined, healthy choices given the challenges you face, choices that provide the greatest return for the least amount of effort.

- *Integrity + Renewal* urges you to proactively manage and refresh your resources and energies so that you maintain healthy growth over time.

- *Integrity + Sustainability* encourages you to build the capabilities and infrastructure for leading with wellth long into the future.

More than just an essential to use in your leadership or business, Integrity and its underlying elements are useful tools for thinking and acting, whether you are part of a project team, coaching the soccer league or hosting a social event. Integrity is simply the foundation for creating long-lasting wellth and effectiveness in whatever you do.

Exercises for Making
Integrity Personal

1 With pen and paper, take 30 minutes to list the values that are important to you, such as honesty, competence, humility, self-assurance, goodness and courage. After you have generated a thorough list, choose the three to five values from which you will commit to consistently leading and living. Make a few notes to yourself about how these values will show up in the ways you treat yourself, your employees, members of your family, nature and so on. Schedule regular times to periodically assess how well you lead and live from these values.

2 Purchase the book, *Now, Discover Your Strengths* (by Marcus Buckingham & Donald Clifton, 2001). Following the instructions in that book, take the online assessment to determine your innate leadership talents. Then, decide how to most productively use these strengths in your role so that you generate a wider, healthier impact as well as less stress in your life and work.

3 Write your obituary. In it, write a few sentences about what the following people say about your life and the contributions you made: your spouse, children, co-workers, boss, employees, neighbors, church leaders and so on. What themes emerged from what these people said? What appeared to be your purpose? What values did you live by? What seemed to be your strengths? Afterwards, consider what changes you can make now so that you live a life that is most significant to you.

4 Ask yourself, *What creates whole health for me?* To support you in asking this question, take the *Personal Wellth Quotient* in Chapter 3. Spending time on routine exercise, eating well, self-care, hobbies, relationships and your spirituality are known to contribute to a healthy person and well-rounded life overall. And, being healthy naturally gives you the energy to lead your business and serve stakeholders, inside and outside the company, more productively. What do you need to do to foster greater health so that you have more energy and wisdom to lead?

Chapter Highlights

- *Rising corporate scandals and a dwindling consumer confidence make leading business with Integrity hot in the public mind.*

- *Integrity is more than ethics. It is about paying attention to the health, wealth and performance of your leadership all at the same time.*

- *Integrity is evident when your* core purpose, enduring values *and* natural strengths *show up in how you lead.*

- *Core purpose, enduring values and natural strengths are three qualities of Integrity that make your leadership and your organization alive and resilient, even in times of market unrest and organizational change.*

- *While competitors can easily imitate your organizational structure, market strategies and business practices, they cannot imitate the DNA of your company, your enduring Integrity.*

- *Businesses structured to operate with Integrity frequently find they enjoy differentiated products and services, intensely loyal customers, an ease in getting work done, streamlined marketing efforts, a stable organizational culture and an energized workforce, and leaders who can make quicker, more mindful decisions.*

- *Integrity is at the heart of* The 7 Essentials[sm]. *Through Integrity and the other essentials, the 21st century leader achieves results with the greatest ease, wellth and sustainability.*

from breakdowns
to breakthroughs

"Often the rapid pace of our lives and work doesn't provide us the opportunity to be in reflective conversations where creative questions and innovative solutions can be explored before reaching key decisions. This dilemma is further reinforced by organizational reward systems in which leaders feel they are paid for fixing problems rather than fostering breakthrough thinking. Between our deep attachment to the answer—any answer—and our anxiety about not knowing, we have inadvertently thwarted our collective capacity for deep creativity and fresh perspectives in the face of the unprecedented challenges we face, both in our own organization and as a global human community."[1]

**Juanita Brown, David Isaacs, Eric Vogt and Nancy Margulies,
organizational consultants**

"A very powerful question may not have an answer at the moment it is asked. It will sit rattling in the mind for days or weeks as the person works on an answer. If the seed is planted, the answer will grow. Questions are alive."[2]

Fran Peavey, social change activist

---

from breakdowns
to breakthroughs

The conversation was tense. It seemed absurd that such smart, well-intentioned people could turn so hostile. But after five hours of unrelenting debate in a small, windowless conference room, these leaders had descended to the pitfalls of anger.

They are the executive team, charged with strategically positioning their telecommunications business for the future. Yet, in a market of wild ups and downs and rollercoaster changes in their workforce to match, these executives have all but surrendered their visionary role, spending the majority of their time arguing about how to keep the business afloat. What is today's conversation? It's about how to react to the latest regulatory guidelines that have hamstrung the company's European sales.

This leadership team is in the middle of a breakdown, a situation that every team finds itself in at one point or another. Their breakdown isn't purely a result of the controversial regulations. It's also about the smaller, yet insidious breakdowns in how they relate to their predicament and to each other. Instead of seeing any benefits they can gain from their thorny situation, they are grappling with the question, *How can we get out of this mess?* (Expletives removed!)

Like many teams, the stance these executives have taken is akin to warfare, battling their breakdown as well as one another to somehow find a solution. Any solution that can get them out of the pain they're in. Well-planned war strategy is how they've always solved their problems before, however taxing this type of strategy may be. Why would they try anything different?

All leaders have business conundrums to solve and emergencies that must be dealt with at once. Yet, most of us get into a habit of immediately responding to breakdowns in the same way every time they appear—and usually that includes a generous dose of judgment, confrontation and struggle. Instead of drawing from our collective intelligence, we bat around individual opinions to see which will win out over the rest. And, by the time we choose which path to take, we act out of anxiety, apathy, or, worse, resentment. We stay mired in this fruitless cycle of managing breakdowns because we never dreamed that *the way we relate to breakdowns* could possibly improve.

21st century leaders and businesses restructure breakdowns into breakthroughs using the transformative power of questions.

The 7 Essentials*sm* employs a more progressive 21st century approach: to restructure breakdowns into breakthroughs using the transformative power of questions.

What Exactly is a Breakdown?

When we consider the word *breakdown*, we are usually thinking of problems that weigh us down. However, we can redefine the concept of a breakdown in a more valuable light. A breakdown is simply a situation that interrupts our comfortable ways of operating, like an unexpected competitor in the market, a surprise visit from a friend or a noise that disrupts your thoughts. Before the breakdown, you are absorbed in your activities; when the breakdown occurs, your unconscious flow of activity is broken (hence the term, *breakdown*). Whether your experience of the breakdown is positive or negative, at least for a moment (and sometimes longer) you are no longer attuned to the flow you were in.

Breakdowns are indispensable. Yet, we frequently don't know how to use them as an avenue for producing wellth.

We often associate breakdowns as negative when we don't know how to profit from them. In these instances, we spend a great deal of energy reacting to breakdowns rather than using them to develop greater personal and collective maturity. Yet, breakdowns are indispensable. We just haven't learned how to use them as an avenue for producing wellth.

A breakdown only causes suffering because of how we respond to it.

Typically, the moment we name something a breakdown, we set in motion a horde of problem-solving resources and activities to fix it. The act of fixing problems rather than fully understanding them is like an involuntary reflex. Our unstated goal is to resume the level of comfort and automatic ease we once knew. We want to make the problem go away quickly and find relief.

What is the unintended consequence of our unstated goal? We give the breakdown a life and momentum of its own; our attention and energies are riveted on reacting to a problem rather than creating the results we want. *Now the breakdown controls us instead of visa versa.* It is our adversary. And, our reactive approach takes a toll on our well-being, our creativity and our productivity. Ironically, we hardly ever study how we relate to breakdowns, nor do we try to relate to them differently. Most of us aren't even sure what that would require.

> **Breakdowns require 21st century leaders to shift their consciousness, ask new questions and redefine reality in more honest and healthier ways.**

For 21st century leaders, breakdowns aren't negative situations at all. They are opportunities for individual or collective learning that are made obvious. Breakdowns serve a critical function in a leader's quest to become healthier and more effective. They starkly reveal, perhaps for the first time, how every person, institution and society can become trapped in certain assumptions and approaches for success,[3] to the loss of other options. Consequently, breakdowns challenge 21st century leaders to reexamine the thinking underneath their decisions, to ask the kinds of questions that take them beyond their comfort zone and to outgrow what they were thinking before. In effect, breakdowns require 21st century leaders to shift their consciousness, ask new questions and redefine reality in more honest and healthier ways.

> **"The first responsibility of a leader is to define reality."[4]**
>
> Max Dupree, Chairman Emeritus of Herman Miller

In fact, to be a progressive 21st century business or leader means knowing how to deal with breakdowns creatively, to anticipate breakdowns before they appear and to *generate* the breakdowns which stimulate innovation and healthy growth. Breakdowns are a chance for people and whole organizations to explore the thinking and actions they've taken so far, recommit to the results they most care about and literally invent how to get there. Breakdowns are like an unforeseen, opening door. When we walk through them mindfully, we become more conscious and capable.

Breakdowns inevitably occur. In this sense, they are predictable. The evolving, dynamic nature of life ripens with complexity and change, so life is also about continual breakdowns and upsets. Employees, organizations, business partnerships and markets are not under our control, and we cannot be prepared for all breakdowns that are bound to happen. Our lack of control makes it all the more imperative that 21st century leaders develop a personal capacity and a business culture in which to respond to and produce breakdowns with wisdom. We must ask the questions we've never asked so that we transform breakdowns into breakthrough innovations and wellth-driven results.

> **To be a progressive 21st century business or leader means knowing how to deal with breakdowns creatively, to anticipate breakdowns before they appear and to generate the breakdowns which stimulate innovation and healthy growth.**

Leading with Questions Rather than Answers

We're not going to eliminate every potential breakdown, and it does no good to ignore their possibility. Therefore, how can we create worthwhile value from the breakdowns that may confront us? One way is to ask productive questions. A good question can literally restructure a breakdown into unforeseen solutions. Because of this, 21st century leaders actively *lead with questions* instead of answers.

We believe that leaders who lead with questions are well ahead in the business game for three reasons:

1 **The answers that we've traditionally used are increasingly outdated.** We are accustomed to showing up with answers to our problems, yet, more often than not, our usual answers no longer get the best results. Either they only work for a short time or they lack relevance and fail us completely. We need answers that can stand up to the complexity of our challenges, and to find those answers, we have to lead with better questions.

2 There are too many answers to choose from. In a world so full of choices, it can be difficult to discern what path to take. We often face conflicting concerns with limited time and energy to spend on any one priority. With the goal to be good leaders, good parents, good partners and good human beings, it's hard to know how to make the best choices right now. What's more, we're acutely aware that no one can make choices for us. We have to find the best answers on our own. Fortunately, finding answers gets easier when we recognize and shape the deeper questions that drive us.

3 The sources of authority that we've used for answers in the past are unable to solve their own problems, much less give us insight into ours. Since the 1960's or even longer, our major institutions have been crumbling. They've lost their sense of purpose and effectiveness. Education, politics, government, big business, religion and healthcare alike have deteriorated and don't keep pace with society's aims. Our key institutions make promises they don't deliver, and we're often left feeling jaded and disillusioned. In some cases, we've given up on our institutions altogether. Many parents choose to home school their kids instead of offering them public education. Countless patients take healthcare into their own hands rather than utilize an impersonal, costly healthcare system. The societal trend is away from conventional religious settings and toward an eclectic, personalized spirituality. Plus, the public is more suspicious of business every day. We no longer solely rely on the institutions we once had faith in to give us the answers to manage our lives and our organizations.

By July 2002, only 21 percent of the American public felt a "great deal of confidence" in the public school system, 14 percent in the medical system, 12 percent in organized labor, 11 percent in the U.S. Congress, and a mere 7 percent in big business.[5]

The bottom line is that on all levels, micro to macro, life is more uncertain than it has ever been. For all our sophisticated analyses, we can't accurately project that the stock market will always go up or that financial returns will always be double digit for a particular industry. For all our hard work at parenting, we can't know for sure that our kids will make good decisions. For all our attempts to eat healthy, we can't be certain that our bodies are getting exactly the nutrients they need. We don't have all the answers.

Nevertheless, we often still behave as if we do. We are more filled with certainty than we are with curiosity. We live in a world of infinite answers more than we do a world of infinite questions.

21st century leaders buck the trend. They know that they don't have control over how the world works, but they do have control over how they think about the world and how they respond to it. As an alternative to trying to control the world with answers, 21st century leaders use questions as a tool to produce less stress, greater ease and wellth for themselves and the systems they influence. They balance their opinions and decisions with questioning, knowing that productive questions are a principal feature of high performing teams and organizations.[6]

21st century leaders also appreciate the personal and social transformations that come through the simple act of questioning. Said best by pioneering social activist, Fran Peavey:[7, 8]

- ☑ "Questioning is a basic tool for rebellion. It breaks open the stagnant hardened shells of the present, and opens up the options that might be explored."

- ☑ "Questioning reveals the profound uncertainty that is embedded deep in all reality beyond the façades of confidence and sureness. It takes this uncertainty towards growth and new possibilities."

- ☑ "Questioning can change your entire life. It can uncover hidden powers and stifled dreams inside of you … things you may have denied for many years."

- ☑ "Questioning can change institutions and entire cultures. It can empower people to create strategies for change."

Using questions, 21st century leaders give rise to a space for discovery in order to enlighten their decisions. Questions are an instrument these leaders apply to think what nobody else has thought before and to get whole organizations and societies to do the same. They value how a powerful question can radically alter even an imminent crisis into 21st century opportunity.

"Discovery consists of seeing what everybody has seen and thinking what nobody has thought." [9]

1937 Nobel Laureate Albert Szent-Gyorgi

When two organizations merged to form the Financial Planning Association (FPA), they shared a similar purpose: to be the community that fosters the value of financial planning and advances the financial profession. However, each organization had its own ideas and particular ways of operating to reach that purpose. Instead of immediately reconciling the discrepancies, leaders from both sides of the newly-formed organization hosted a series of café-styled events focused on a single strategic question: *What one question, if addressed, would change the future of financial planning?* As people worked with this question, they were able to rise above their differences and surface totally new aspirations for the field of financial planning that wouldn't have otherwise emerged. Today, the leaders sponsor a variety of question-directed events for their financial planners, brokers and organizational managers in order to continually create a healthy future for FPA and to maintain its collaborative culture. [10]

21st century leaders know that only the generative force *between* people is great enough to resolve our contemporary challenges. They use questions to tap into this generative force connecting us to an impetus that's bigger than any person, group or nation alone.

As a 21st century leader, you can learn to lead with questions instead of answers as well, using two primary methods:

■ **Live in the questions**—This is the ability to hold a question with your self or others without thinking you have all the answers or even that you're *supposed* to. For instance, after envisioning your future, you might wonder, *How will we realize this vision of success?* But instead of answering that question right away, you agree to sit with it for a period of time. You choose to remain receptive and notice what solutions naturally appear, to pay attention with new eyes. *Living in* the question draws on the depth of wisdom people possess when they have ample space in which to incubate, listen and reflect.

> Living in the questions is the ability to hold a question without thinking you have all the answers or even that you're supposed to.

■ **Work with questions**—This is the skill of proactively using questions to provoke constructive shifts in thinking and action. It builds on the innate desire people have to actively use their fertile imaginations as part of a positive solution. For example, when stuck in one view of a problem, you might ask, *What else might be occurring here?* Or, *How else could we interpret this?* to prod your team toward non-conventional perspectives. When you *work with* questions, the questions raised by you and others create motion toward productive, wellth-directed change.

> Working with questions is the skill of proactively using questions to provoke constructive shifts in thinking and action.

The power of questioning comes from knowing *how* and *when* to use each method for living in and working with questions. These methods help you draw on people's rationality, their emotions and their intuitions so that you capture their full range of creative intelligence.

The 7 Essentials^{sm} offers a variety of questions that you can live in and work with to help you contribute to healthy results. Let's examine how you can better relate to and use questions to enhance your 21st century leadership.

21st Century Leadership in Action

Living in and Working with Questions

Take two to three consecutive days to evaluate yourself as a leader in action:

- *Consider your projects, conversations, meetings and internal dialogue. Do you ask questions or do you tend to show up with answers?*

- *When are you more inclined to* live in *questions? When are you more inclined to* work with *questions?*

- *How well do you* live in *and* work with *questions as a tool for innovating, learning and sustaining change? How frequently do you employ these methods?*

- *In what situations could you practice* living in *and* working with *questions in order to achieve better results? For instance, this could be with a team you lead, your family or a business partnership. Choose situations that are safe to practice something new and that will stretch you. Decide now how you will experiment with* living in *and* working with *questions, and notice the results.*

For many leaders, living in and working with questions is easier said than done. By and large, traditional management training and organizational kudos teach us to jump to quick fixes, reducing the room we need to ask better questions and design better solutions altogether. We frequently are measured (and, just as frequently, we measure our selves and others) on having airtight answers, which blocks us from probing our problems enough to discover good questions.

Plus, not any old question will do. In fact, some questions shut down possibilities instead of opening new insights and learning. Like the executive story that began this chapter, many of us fall into the trap of driving our responses to breakdowns with unproductive questions, such as, *How can we get out of this mess?* even when we aren't in a dire crises. Asked over and over again, this kind of question compels us to act and react from problem to problem, like a bee feverishly buzzing from flower to flower. We become problem-seekers rather than aspiration-achievers. A more powerful question we could ask might be: *Given our goals, how can we navigate this challenge so that we create sustained benefit now and in the future?* This question is a wholly new starting point from which to make leadership decisions.

Living in and working with questions requires 21st century leaders to use questions in light of the ultimate results and well-being they most want. We consider these questions *strategic*.

A New Tool for Your 21st Century Leadership Toolkit: *Strategic Questions*

Strategic questions are the types of questions that best deliver wellth-driven performance and results. They are another tool to add to your 21st century leadership toolkit. *The 7 Essentials[sm]* framework is chocked full of such questions. Before examining this framework however, let's discuss the characteristics of strategic questions:[11,12]

- *They value and enhance the Integrity of the person or group being questioned as well as the questioner.* Strategic questions help people and entire systems get to know themselves better, whether that's to understand their internal ways of thinking, the values that guide their decisions or the effects of their behaviors. In this way, it is questions—not answers—that enable individuals and groups to enhance well-being and performance on their own.

- *They have a clear and constructive intent.* Strategic questions are asked in the spirit of true inquiry, where the intent behind the question is generative, for example: to truly understand another's point of view, to foster collaborative insights, to imagine possibilities, to evaluate progress or to create momentum for positive action.

- *They are growth oriented.* Strategic questions tap into the underlying ideals and goals that truly motivate people to create and maintain results they care about and to develop new wisdom along the way.

- *They invite other people to engage their minds, hearts and actions.* Strategic questions create a neutral or common ground within which people can think, share points of view, build bridges between each other, co-create knowledge and implement plans in concert.

- *They foster innovation.* Strategic questions broaden the field of vision so that people see possibilities they couldn't see before. This helps people connect and experiment with new ideas which, as appropriate, can be profitably put into practice.

- *They get to the essence.* Strategic questions search for the deeper truth of what is really going on, and they give people a different frame from which to perceive their situation. They are a mechanism for unlearning what people currently know as much as for learning something new. Plus, strategic questions help people revisit the fundamental assumptions on which their thinking and decisions are based.

- *They create movement.* Strategic questions cause people to act in service to their internal desires rather than react under pressure.

- *They are a much-needed pause before making a decision.* Strategic questions provide an opportunity for people to reflect privately as well as publicly. Instead of plunging into a potentially harmful decision, this chance to reflect fosters a depth of insight, meaning and commitment behind decisions, ingredients that help make decisions last.

Strategic questions are dynamic. They reinforce movement and growth versus stagnation. They also shift our perception about the nature of our challenges, and they give our strategies for change greater focus and long-term effectiveness. Thus, strategic questions can be utilized well in every phase of a process to plan, activate and sustain healthy results, personally and professionally.

The conscious use of strategic questioning isn't as clearcut as it may seem. Quite often we ask questions that lack mindfulness, times where we are unaware of our intentions. You'll know you are coming from these non-strategic ways when you ask questions mainly to: reconfirm a point of view you already hold, reinforce an approach you've used in the past, build resistance or overanalyze a situation. You may also find yourself using questions to blame, fix, interrogate, manipulate or avoid conflict with someone else. Plus,

> "Find the right questions. You don't invent the answers, you "reveal" the answers." [13]
>
> Jonas Salk, physician

you may use questions non-strategically to give the impression that you care about something or someone when you really don't, to put someone on the defensive, or to withdraw from a conversation so that you can hide your ideas and opinions. [14,15] Ultimately, none of these approaches for asking questions create positive, enduring effects for you or anyone else.

With this in mind, when is a good time for you to employ strategic questions?

- ☑ **When you are stuck in a complex problem or when the solution to your complex problem appears obvious.** Don't fool yourself! Complex problems require you to dig a little deeper if you want solutions that alleviate the problem and prevent it from returning. When things get complex, that's your signal to ask strategic questions instead of jumping to the quickest solution.

- ☑ **When you are fixated on one particular solution to the expense of all others.** Instead of being close-minded, use strategic questions to open you up to alternatives. This makes you better equipped to choose actions of leverage and ingenuity.

- ☑ **When you realize that you don't understand the situation you are in.** Strategic questions give you a device for exploring totally new ways of looking at your realities. They bring to consciousness the insights that can assist you in sorting out the situation.

☑ **When emotions are running high and the environment is volatile.** A reactive environment usually breeds non-strategic thinking and decisions. In this atmosphere, you are likely to reproduce or exacerbate your problems if you don't start asking strategic questions.

☑ **When you notice that the questions being asked already have the answers hidden with them.** This tendency is common, yet it predisposes you to a pre-planned course of action instead of helping you discover any new options. Put your foregone conclusions aside and redesign your questions so that they are strategic.

21st Century Leadership in Action

Asking Strategic Questions

For two to three days, examine the types of questions you ask in your conversations and inner dialogue:

- *What is generally the intent behind your questions? For example, are your questions designed to defend your position, to debate a point of view or to understand the ideas of others? What intentions characterize your questions? Where is this useful for you and where is it eroding your productivity?*

- *Consider the criteria in this chapter that describe strategic questions. Are your questions strategic? If not, what might you do to shift toward strategic questions in your leadership and in life?*

- *Choose a situation that seems stuck or unproductive. Is this a situation where you might apply strategic questioning? If so, craft a strategic question using the characteristics mentioned in this chapter. Ask the question to the appropriate people (including yourself) and notice the results.*

Strategic Questions in *The 7 Essentials*^{sm}

Now that you have a handle on the characteristics of strategic questions, let's talk about specific strategic questions that make up *The 7 Essentials.*^{sm} This leadership framework contains questions particularly designed for 21st century leaders who want to achieve and sustain success in the healthiest manner possible. It assumes that, by nature, people are already capable of creative insights and productive change, and that this energy can be channeled by using powerful questions.

In Chapter 5, we mentioned the central question that vitalizes this leadership framework:

How can success be achieved and sustained in a healthy, life-enhancing way?

Already, this focusing question biases the questions that follow it toward the goal to create total health and sustainability, the fundamental driver of the 21st century leader and organization. This question is an unconventional, yet more powerful, wellth-directed orientation from which to begin your process of inquiry. It is the core energy for generative change, compassionate action and conscious growth.

Each of the seven essentials provides additional questions that can lead to creative and sustainable solutions. The sample questions below are written for groups, such as a department or a culture ready to achieve new results. However, by changing the pronoun to 'I,' they can easily be utilized by individuals as well.

The Essential

Integrity

What is our core purpose? Why do we exist?

What are our values? How will we use these values to guide our thinking and behavior?

What are our strengths? How will we capitalize on our strengths to achieve our aspirations with excellence?

What helps us succeed naturally? How will we optimize our success?

What are healthy limits to our growth? How will we respect those limits?

Aspiration

What results do we want to create?

What results are we getting now?

Which of our desired results generate the widest span of benefit to our selves and others?

Innovation

To achieve the results we want, what experiments could we try? How will our values and strengths shape our experiments?

What innovations have we 'put a lid on' and, by doing so, how may we be preventing our own health and performance?

How will we learn from what we do?

Simplicity

How will we focus our actions?

How can we achieve our goals with the greatest ease as well as a minimum amount of energy or resources?

Strategic Questions

Movement

What are the intentions behind our actions?

What may be the consequences of our actions? What relationships may be affected?

How might we act mindfully and collaboratively in our decisions and actions?

How will we act in a way that benefits our relationships as well as our selves?

Sustainability

What routines, practice or structures will we put in place so that our preferred results endure over time?

How will we sustain momentum for our change?

How will we factor in the peaks, valleys, plateaus and delays that are a natural part of the change process?

What capabilities will we cultivate so that we move into the future with wisdom?

Renewal

How will we replenish the energies and resources that we use?

How will we support healing that which needs to be healed?

How will we continually refresh our selves and enable our constituencies to do the same?

Not surprisingly, some of the most influential questions are also the simplest. They just need to be asked, especially during those times when our tendency to react kicks into high gear. Plus, some of the questions above require us to reply, "I don't know." This admission naturally urges us to search deeper for answers that will be more effective for our circumstances rather than concern ourselves with looking good, protecting our turf or utilizing other defensive routines that thwart our progress. Plainly, strategic questioning requires a great deal of inner fortitude and courage.

21st Century Leadership in Action

Applying Questions from The 7 Essentials^{sm}

Select a situation in which you would like to achieve and sustain a new quality of results than you have before. This situation may be personal or work-related. Using the table above, ask the strategic questions of *The 7 Essentials^{sm}*. Give yourself time to receptively live in and actively work with each question. Notice what new insights and options come to enable greater wellth and effectiveness in your situation.

The strategic questions of *The 7 Essentials^{sm}* apply at any level—for personal gain, for group planning, to guide a business partnership or for worldwide change. For example, Mary recently went to the doctor to repair a torn meniscus in her knee. In preparation of her operation, the doctor asked, "Do you participate in any physical, mental, emotional or spiritual practices that might impact your surgery or facilitate your healing process?" Mary was stunned! In her years of engaging conventional health care, this kind of question was unprecedented. It was a strategic question at the heart of Renewal. For

"Try to love the questions themselves, like locked rooms... Live the questions now. Perhaps you will then, gradually, live along some distant day, into the answer."[16]

Rainer Marie Rilke, poet

the first time ever, Mary felt like she had been addressed as a whole person instead of a symptom. Plus, in answering the questions, she became more aware of what it would take during and beyond the surgery to make her healing process a little easier. Not only did the doctor get the information he needed, but Mary had now become a healing partner instead of a patient, a fundamentally different and more influential role in restoring her health.

That's the transformative power of using simple yet strategic questions from *The 7 Essentials.*^{sm}

The 7 Essentials^{sm} **Questions in Your Work as a 21st Century Leader**

As a 21st century leader, asking strategic questions from *The 7 Essentials*^{sm} can change your relationship both with your circumstances today and with the future. These questions also can change your relationship with others so that your interactions are more about shared commitment than they are about compliance. Most importantly, these questions turned inward as a self-coaching device can change your relationship with your self so that you become a healthier, more productive leader not only in your work, but in your life overall.

It's easy to react to our problems and differences as breakdowns that we must conquer. However, devising answers that have power over people and situations is an approach that's long exhausted its value. It's an exclusive approach, and the world is overdue for something inclusive and fresh. The more challenging and exciting work of today is to discover—in the middle of even our largest breakdowns—the deeper passions that people will come together to achieve and sustain. This is your work as a 21st century leader. It is your opportunity to help others turn breakdowns into breakthrough results through the transformative power of questions.

Exercises for Turning Breakdowns into Breakthroughs using the Transformative Power of Questions

1 Choose a specific project that you want to address. Use the strategic questions from *The 7 Essentials*^{sm} framework to help you clarify your goals and actions in this project. (Tailor those questions to your project as needed.) Determine how and when you will use these questions to give your project ongoing support.

2 Craft two to three compelling questions that enable you to operate from a wellth-centric orientation. What few questions could you ask yourself each day so that you remember to think, decide and act for the higher success of your self and others? How will you live in and work with these questions? Write these questions down and review them each day.

3 For at least one week, pretend that your job as a 21st century leader is primarily to ask strategic questions. Ask questions from *The 7 Essentials*^{sm} framework any and every time you can in meetings, conversations and projects. Notice the effects this seems to have on you and others as well, plus the results you strive to produce.

Chapter Highlights

- *All leaders have breakdowns to solve. Yet, most of us get into a habit of immediately responding to every breakdown the same way. We get stuck in a reactive cycle of managing breakdowns because we never dream that the way we think about breakdowns could possibly be improved.*

- *The 7 Essentials^{sm} helps you restructure breakdowns into breakthroughs through the transformative power of questions.*

- *For many leaders, leading with questions rather than answers is easier said than done. By and large, traditional management training and organizational kudos teach us to jump to quick fixes, reducing the breathing room we need to ask better questions and design better solutions.*

- *21st century leaders know how to live in and proactively work with strategic questions to produce healthier innovations, decisions and wellth-driven success.*

the end is the beginning

"Welcome to the Age of Possibility. Welcome to a world in which reality is whatever we make it, a world in which you both can and must immerse yourself in your own possibilities, a world in which you—you the person, you the business, you the organization, you the government, and you the society—can write your own story and walk into it and become whatever it is you imagine yourself becoming... You really are free, and as all truly free people are, you really are responsible. Fail to build your own future, and someone is going to build one for you, whether you want it or not. Fail to bind all the disparately emerging futures within your organization—be it a company, school, government, or family—to a shared set of goals, and its future will be forfeit, too."[1]

The Visionary's Handbook

"The Buddha compared the universe to a vast net woven of a countless variety of brilliant jewels, each with a countless number of facets. Each jewel reflects in itself every other jewel in the net and is, in fact, one with every other jewel... Everything is inextricably interrelated: We come to realize that we are responsible for everything we do, say, or think, responsible in fact for ourselves, everyone and everything else, and the entire universe."[2]

Professor Sogyal Rinpoche, author

"Business is inherently difficult. That's why management is the highest spiritual calling I know."[3]

M. Scott Peck, author

---

the end is the beginning

21st century leaders evolve a global culture
of health and sustainability

In a world beleaguered with complex problems, the promise of 21st century leadership is a healthier global culture for business and civilization.

We don't have to look very far to see the crises we face. Our predicaments don't arise only on an international scale that's distant and hard to fathom; closer to home, complex problems are evident within our communities and personal lives every day in at least three major arenas: [4]

- **A crisis of the commons**—challenges in how we share and use land, air, water, space and other resources, such as research, TV and radio airwaves and the Internet, to meet our needs today and in the future

- **A crisis of humanity**—enormous disparities in wealth, education, health, freedoms and human rights, as well as prejudices, traditions and institutions that keep those disparities alive

- **A crisis of control**—powerful instruments, such as in biotechnology, trade and the media, often without the prudence to use these instruments wisely

Underneath these three crises lies a fourth: *a crisis of meaning and values*. We often unknowingly live our lives and run our organizations obsessed by motivations that will never provide the ultimate security and fulfillment we seek. Biased by the drive for wealth and material things, our modern profit-centric values have bestowed us with many possessions, yet little sustained health or satisfaction. We become further trapped by tolerating our current circumstances with apathy, or worse, as if we are helpless. We sabotage ourselves by not challenging the values that sustain our predicaments.

The Crossroads of 21st Century Leadership

Are our present crises a problem? Sure, and they become even more menacing when we dwell on them without keeping a larger perspective of our evolutionary path in mind. Our crises are of our creation, anchored in values that have directed our life and leadership so far. Nonetheless, we stand at a crossroads: we can try to fix our crises using values of the past, or we can use our crises as the impetus to evolve healthier values and practices for a wellth-generating future. Consciously creating a healthier future is the heart and soul of *The 7 Essentials*.^{sm}

> **As 21st century leaders, we can try to fix our crises using values of the past, or we can use our crises as the impetus to evolve healthier values and practices for a wellth-generating future.**

In truth, our crossroads is the contemporary stage for the profound, courageous and compassionate choices emerging from 21st century leaders and their companies. Because whether manifested as eco-friendly products, ethical management, conscientious marketing, corporate responsibility, social entrepreneurship or win-win alliances, the central theme of this kind of leadership is unswerving: 21st century leaders continually strive to evolve new values and behavioral systems that solve and transcend the basic problems of humankind.[6] These leaders are on a never-ending quest to transform business into an additive force for well-being and to stretch other arenas of society (such as healthcare, government and education) to do the same. This turns business priorities

"Let us widen our perspective to include the well being of the whole world and its future generations in our vision of economics and business." [5]

The Dalai Lama, spiritual leader

inside-out; instead of profit being the highest concern, it is in service to the goals of the health and sustainability of life.

From 21st Century Leadership Theory to 21st Century Action

As you've examined throughout this book, 21st century leaders are inventing healthier theories for the entity of business to rest on, while they draw from and celebrate the wisdom of theories past. Plus, given the global reach of contemporary businesses large and small, these leaders use corporations as a mechanism for spreading healthier options for living and working far and wide.

> "Creating a new theory is not like destroying an old barn and erecting a skyscraper in its place. It is rather like climbing a mountain, gaining new and wider views, discovering unexpected connections between our starting point and its rich environment."[7]
>
> Albert Einstein

21st century leaders are attempting to align their lives, their relationships and their companies with the unfolding, creative fabric of human and natural life. They relentlessly ask the question *What are we creating for?* to ensure that what they produce and how they produce it embraces the health of the whole.

Said best by Richard Florida, 21st century leaders consider how to use creative intelligence toward positive aims:

> "Creativity is not an unmitigated good but a human capacity that can be applied to many different ends. We must carefully consider the ends to which we direct our creativity. It is a precious asset not to be squandered trivially and a powerful force to be harnessed and directed with careful consideration of all its possible consequences. …what kind of society do we want to bequeath to coming generations?"[8]

21st century leaders are learning how to consciously use power, whether that power is in the form of financial wealth, corporate reach, title, influence or personal presence. By using power wisely, they are setting the stage for new freedoms and a higher quality of collaboration and resourcefulness to come to fore in the world theater.

Through holistic decision-making frameworks, such as *The 7 Essentials*,[sm] 21st century leaders are reconnecting to the original purpose of business: *to build something great and to be of service to the world.*[10] Through their wisdom, visions and deeds, these leaders are creating new, integral reference points of compassion, courage, wellness, humility, acceptance, love and balanced growth from which to measure business decisions and performance. They are radically raising the bar for leadership and business success.

"Freedom is actually a bigger game than power. Power is about what you can control. Freedom is about what you can unleash."[9]

Harriet Rubin, author and former Editor at Doubleday/Currency

---

In the Swedish language, the oldest term for business means *nourishment for life*. And, the 3,000 year old Chinese characters for business translate in English to *life* or *live* and *meaning.*[11]

Perhaps most remarkably, 21st century leaders are crafting a global culture of health and sustainability that's building its own momentum. They are collectively elevating a world-centric, wellth-driven human consciousness, where health and sustainability is endeavored for its own sake rather than because of moral, legal, political or commercial obligations. 21st century leaders are part of a worldwide sea change in mindfulness, where personal and corporate visions of success are better matched to the biological and social realities of human connectedness.

An Invitation to 21st Century Leadership

As this book comes to a close, you may already realize that its end is really just the beginning. It's the beginning of a healthier, more holistic way to lead your life and your company as well as to generatively affect the lives of others, should you choose to step onto the 21st century leadership path. It's an invitation, available to you, awaiting your personal decision.

Know that this kind of leadership is not a job for the meek. But, it is a chosen and meaningful existence by a growing number of leaders and companies that have learned: *this kind of leadership keeps calling until the call is answered.* The call now before you is:

How will you express 21st century leadership?

21st century leadership is an evolutionary leap into a whole different way of leading, unlike the leadership orientations anyone has known before. As authors and leaders, we are continuously learning about the enlightened experiments and methods 21st century leaders all across the world are applying to set a new example of wellth-driven success. We've learned that this leadership is empowered when leaders collaborate and learn with one another. As a result, we invite you to share your 21st century leadership stories with us so that we can share your wisdom with others. (You'll find our contact information in the Appendix.)

> "...without a global revolution in the sphere of human consciousness, nothing will change for the better in the sphere of our being as human." [12]
>
> Vaclav Havel, former Czech President

Many blessings on your leadership journey.

appendix

"The reality of the contemporary world is complex. It is a fantastic mix of tragedy, irreparable misfortune, apathy, prejudices, and ignorance, plus dynamism, selflessness, hope, and intelligence. The future may be even more tragic. Or it may be more worthy of human beings—better and more intelligent. Or it may not be at all. It depends on all of us—people in every country in the world It depends on our wisdom, our freedom from illusion and prejudice, our readiness to work, to practice intelligent austerity, and on our kindness and breadth as human beings."[1]

Andrei Sakharov, physicist and human rights activist

appendix

additional resources to support your learning

References by Chapter

Chapter 1

1. Merton, Thomas. Seeds. Ed. Robert Inchausti. Boston: Shambhala, 2002.
2. Paulson, Daryl. Competitive Business, Caring Business: An Integral Business Perspective for the 21st Century. New York: Paraview Press, 2002.
3. Collins, Jim. "Built to Flip," Fast Company May (2002).
4. Kelly, Marjorie. The Divine Right of Capital. San Francisco: Berrett-Koehler, 2001.
5. World Health Organization. "The World Health Report 2002: Reducing Risks, Promoting Healthy Life." (2002).
6. Ibis.
7. Cincotta, Richard and Robert Engelman. Nature's Place: Human Population and the Future of Biological Diversity. Population Action International, 2000.
8. Vital Signs 2002. New York: W.W. Norton & Company, 2002: 82.
9. Elgin, Duane and Coleen LeDrew. Global Consciousness Change: Indicators on an Emerging Paradigm. San Anselmo: Millennium Project, 1997 <www.awakeningearth.org/reports/gcc/pdf>.
10. Ibis.
11. Vital Signs 2002. New York: W.W. Norton & Company, 2002: 60.
12. World Messenger. Website. <www.worldmessenger.com> (2003).
13. IMF World Economic Outlook. Report. April (2003) <www.imf.org>.
14. Vital Signs 2002. New York: W.W. Norton & Company, 2002.
15. Tyson, Laura. "The New Economy is Dead. Long Live the New Economy." Essay. World Economic Forum Annual Meeting. (2003).
16. Petzinger, Thomas. "A New Model for the Nature of Business: It's Alive!," Wall Street Journal. 26 Feb 1999.
17. Elgin, Duane and Coleen LeDrew. Global Consciousness Change: Indicators on an Emerging Paradigm. San Anselmo: Millennium Project, 1997 <www.awakeningearth.org/reports/gcc/pdf>.
18. Beck, Don and Chris Cowan. Spiral Dynamics: Mastering Values, Leadership and Change. Malden: Blackwell Publishing, 1996.
19. Elgin, Duane and Coleen LeDrew. Global Consciousness Change: Indicators on an Emerging Paradigm. San Anselmo: Millennium Project, 1997 <www.awakeningearth.org/reports/gcc/pdf>.

Chapter 2

1. Roddick, Anita. "The Revolutionary Eccentric." Hope Jul/Aug 38 (2003) 12.
2. Coyote, Peter. "The Arts." Imagine: What American Could be in the 21st Century. Ed. Marianne Williamson. New York: Daybreak, 2000.
3. Branfman, Fred. "Legacies." Imagine: What American Could be in the 21st Century. Ed. Marianne Williamson. New York: Daybreak, 2000.
4. Ray, Paul and Sherry Ruth Anderson. The Cultural Creatives: How 50 Million People are Changing the World. New York: Crown Publishing Group, 2000.

5. Natural Marketing Institute. "Understanding the LOHAS Consumer Report™". (2003).

6. Ibis.

7. Badiner, Allan Hunt. Mindfulness in the Marketplace. Berkeley: Parallax Press, 2002.

8. Wackernagel, Matthis. "Framing the Sustainability Crisis: Getting from Concern to Action." Research Paper. Sustainable Development Research Initiative, Oct (1997) <www.sdri.ubc.ca>.

9. Search engine on <www.amazon.com>, Nov 2003.

10. Marketing Intelligence Service, Ltd. "Build a Better Mousetrap: 2002 New Product Innovations of the Year." (2002).

11. Hartman, H. Marketing in the Soul Age: Building Lifestyle Worlds. Bellevue: The Hartman Group, 2001.

12. Natural Marketing Institute. "Understanding the LOHAS Consumer Report™". (2003).

13. Ibis.

14. Garcia, A. "The Tao Index Rose Today…," LOHAS Journal 2:4 (2001).

15. Cortese, Amy. "They Care About the World (and They Shop, Too)." New York Times 20 July (2003).

16. Natural Marketing Institute. "Understanding the LOHAS Consumer Report™". (2003).

17. Pink, Dan. Free Agent Nation. New York: Warner Books, 2001.

18. Florida, Richard. "The New American Dream." Washington Monthly 35.2 (2003) 26.

19. Neal, J.A. "Work as Service to the Divine," American Behavioral Scientist 43:8 (2000).

20. Moore, Thomas. Care of the Soul: A Guide for Cultivating Depth and Sacredness in Everyday Life. New York: Perennial Publishers, 1994.

21. Pink, Dan. Free Agent Nation. New York: Warner Books, 2001.

22. Florida, Richard. The Rise of the Creative Class and How It's Transforming Work, Leisure, Community and Everyday Life. New York: Basic Books, 2002.

23. Harman, Willis. Global Mind Change: The Promise of the 21st Century. San Francisco: Berrett-Koehler Publishers, 1998.

24. Belkin, Lisa. "The Opt-Out Revolution." The New York Times 26 Oct 2003.

25. Florida, Richard. The Rise of the Creative Class and How It's Transforming Work, Leisure, Community and Everyday Life. New York: Basic Books, 2002.

26. Ibis, p. 249.

27. Ibis, p. 249.

28. Preston, Lynelle. "Sustainability at Hewlett-Packard: From Theory to Practice." California Management Review 43:3 Spring (2001).

29. Silicon Valley Toxics Coalition. "Poison PCs/Toxic TVs." Report. <www.svtc.org> (2003).

30. Vital Signs 2002. New York: W.W. Norton & Company, 2002: 60.

31. Underwood, R. "Radicals for Responsibility." Fast Company May (2002).

32. "Business Case for Corporate Citizenship." Report. Arthur D. Little <www.adl.com> (2002).

33. Hawley, H. "Surveying Corporate Environmental and Social Reporting," The Ethical Corporation Magazine Feb (2002).

34. Cairncross, Frances. "Tough at the Top." The Economist 23 Oct (2003).

35. Kennedy, Ellen. "The LOHAS Advantage." Presentation. The Natural Market Trends LOHAS Conference. Colorado, 18 June 2003.

36. Wilber, Ken. A Brief History of Everything. Boston: Shambhala Publications, 2000.

37. Pralahad, C.K. Quote from <www.edgewalkers.com> (2003).

38. Meadows, Donella. "Which Future?" In Context: A Quarterly of Humane Sustainable Culture 43 Winter (1995-96).

39. Kiley, David. "Zingerman's Took the Road Less Traveled to Success." USA Today Wed 1 Oct (2003).

40. Inayat Khan, Hazrat . The Art of Being and Becoming. (originally published as Personality: The Art of Being and Becoming) New Lebanon: Omega Publications, 1990.

Chapter 3

1. Nattrass Brian and Mary Altomare. The Natural Step for Business. BC: New Society Publishers, 2001: 13-14.

2. Payutto, Ven. P.A. "Buddhist Perspectives on Economic Concepts." Mindfulness in the Marketplace. Ed. Allan Hunt Badiner. Berkeley: Pallalax Press, 2002.

3. American Heritage Dictionary. Second College Edition. Boston: Houghton Mifflin Company, 1985.

4. Underwood, R. "Radicals for Responsibility." Fast Company May (2002).

5. Worldwatch Institute. "World's Biggest Consumers Hold New Hope for Environment." Report. 24 July 2003.

6. Grayson, David and Adrian Hodges. Everybody's Business: Managing Risks and Opportunities in Today's Global Society. London: Dorling Kindserley Press, 2002.

7. Ibis.

8. Corporate Responsibility Story about The Coca-Cola Company. World Economic Forum, 2003.

9. Bennis, Warren, Jagdish Parikh and Ronnie Essem. Beyond Leadership: Balancing Economics, Ethics and Ecology. Cambridge: Blackwell Business, 1996: 291.

10. Kramer, Robert. "The Harder They Fall." Harvard Business Review 81:10 Oct (2003).

11. World Economic Forum. Harvard Study of Stakeholder Balanced Companies (2003).

12. Ray, Paul. "LOHAS and the Emerging Economy: Structural Changes." LOHAS Conference, Colorado, June (2003).

13. Ibis.

14. Stigson, Bjorn. "Walking the Talk—The Business Case for Sustainable Development." Conference. World Business Council for Sustainable Development. 7 May (2003).

15. "Globalisation of the Organic Food Industry." Organic Monitor 14 July <www.organicmonitor.com> (2003).

16. Bennis, Warren, Jagdish Parikh and Ronnie Essem. Beyond Leadership: Balancing Economics, Ethics and Ecology. Cambridge: Blackwell Business, 1996: 23.

17. "Pick Your Poison: NC Exec Struggles to do the Right Thing." Continuum 17:23 World Business Academy. 29 Oct (2003).

18. Ibis.
19. Pelletier, Kenneth. <u>Sound Mind, Sound Body: A New Model For Lifelong Health</u>. New York: Simon & Schuster Adult Publishing Group, 1994.
20. Shell International. "People and Connections: Global Scenarios to 2020." Report. <www.shell.com> (2002).

Chapter 4

1. Senge, Peter, Art Kleiner, Charlotte Roberts, Richard Ross, George Roth and Bryan Smith. <u>The Dance of Change: The Challenges of Sustaining Momentum in Learning</u>. New York: Doubleday Publishing, 1999.
2. Daft, Doug. Speech. Brandeis University International Business School. 13 Nov (2003).
3. Brian Nattrass and Mary Altomare. <u>The Natural Step for Business</u>. BC: New Society Publishers, 2001.
4. Sheehan, George. "Why Do I Run?" <u>Runner's World</u> Dec (2003): 61.
5. Chua, Amy. "Making the World Safe for Markets." <u>Harvard Business Review</u>. Aug (2003).
6. Meadows, Donella. "Which Future?" <u>In Context: A Quarterly of Humane Sustainable Culture</u> 43 Winter (1995-96).
7. Forrestor, Jay. <u>Principles of Systems</u>. Waltham: Pegasus Communications, 1968.
8. Senge, Peter, Art Kleiner, Charlotte Roberts, Richard Ross, George Roth and Bryan Smith. <u>The Dance of Change: The Challenges of Sustaining Momentum in Learning</u>. New York: Doubleday Publishing, 1999.
9. Kauffman, Draper. <u>Systems 1: An Introduction to Systems Thinking</u>. Future Systems, 1980.
10. Cairncross, Frances. "Tough at the Top." <u>The Economist</u> 23 Oct (2003).
11. Senge, Peter, Art Kleiner, Charlotte Roberts, Richard Ross, George Roth and Bryan Smith. <u>The Dance of Change: The Challenges of Sustaining Momentum in Learning</u>. New York: Doubleday Publishing, 1999: 7.
12. Ibis.
13. Ibis, 10.
14. "Merck Earns Highest Rating in Ethics Study." <u>About Merck</u> <www.merck.com> (2003).
15. Hansen, Mark and Robert Allen. <u>The One Minute Millionaire</u>. New York: Harmony Books, 2002.
16. Lear, Norman. Chairman and CEO, Act III Communications and Founder of Business Enterprise Trust. Quoted at <www.davender.com> (2003).
17. Morse, Gardiner. "Bottom-Up Economics." <u>Harvard Business Review</u> Aug (2003): 18-20.

Chapter 5

1. Einstein, Albert. Quoted in <u>Quantum Reality: Beyond the New Physics</u>. By Nick Herbert. New York: Anchor/Doubleday, 1987: 250.
2. Crooke, Michael. "The Integration of Environmental Activism, Social Integrity and Healthy Financial Performance at Patagonia." Natural Business Market Trends Conference. Colorado, June (2003).

3. Petzinger, Thomas. "A New Model for the Nature of Business: It's Alive!," Wall Street Journal. 26 Feb 1999.

4. Holmes, Ernest. Science of Mind. New York: The Putnam Publishing Group, 1997.

5. Holmes, Ernest. Living the Science of Mind. Eight edition. Marina del Ray: DeVorss & Company, 1999.

6. Capra, Frijof. The Hidden Connections: Integrating the Biological, Cognitive and Social Dimensions of Life into a Science of Sustainability. New York: Doubleday Publishing, 2002: 14.

7. Ibis.

8. Schneider, Michael. A Beginner's Guide to Constructing the Universe: The Mathematical Archetypes of Nature, Art and Science. New York: Harper Perennial, 1995.

9. The Byrds. Turn! Turn! Turn!. 1966 Song. Lyrics. <www.lyrics.com> (2003) .

10. Master's Study Bible. Nashville: Holman Bible Publishers, 1981.

11. Korten, David. "The Post-Corporate World." Yes! A Journal of Positive Futures (2002). Reprinted as "Local Living Economies vs. The Suicide Economy," In Business Jul/Aug (2002).

Chapter 6

1. Fuller, R. Buckminster with Jerome Agel and Quentin Fiore. I Seem To Be a Verb. New York: Bantam Books, 1970.

2. Visions of a Better World. Peace Messenger Initiative of the United Nations. Eds. Jagdish Chander Hassija and Mohini Panjabi. The Brahma Kumaris World Spiritual University, 1994.

3. Sanger, David and Richard Oppell. "Senate Unanimously Passes Corporate Reform Measure." New York Times 16 July 2002.

4. Simonetta, Joe. "The Bottom Line." ViewPoint Newsletter. World Business Academy (2002).

5. American Heritage Dictionary. Second College Edition. Boston: Houghton Mifflin Company, 1985.

6. Bennis, Warren. Quoted in New Traditions in Business: Spirit and Leadership in the 21st Century. By John Renesch. New York: Prima Lifestyles, 1992.

7. Buckingham, Marcus and Donald Clifton. Now, Discover Your Strengths. Toronto: Free Press, 2001.

8. Buddha, Gautama. Quoted in True Work: Doing What you Love and Loving What You Do. By Michael and Justine Toms. New York: Harmony/Bell Tower, 1999.

9. Chopra, Deepek. Quoted in Making a Life, Making a Living. By Mark Albion. New York: Warner Business Books, 2000: 2.

10. Cashman, Kevin. LeaderSource, Inc. <www.leadersource.com> (2003).

11. Hutchens, David. The Lemming Dilemma. Pegasus Communications, Boston, 2000.

12. Ibis.

13. Garland, Judy. Quoted in Simple Abundance: A Daybook of Comfort and Joy. Sarah Ban Breathnack. New York: Warner Books, 1995: 31.

14. O'Brien, William. The Soul of Corporate Leadership. Innovations in Management Series. Waltham: Pegasus Communications, 1998.

15. Ibis.

16. Nussbaum, Martha. Quoted in article by Harriet Rubin. "Global Values in a Local World." Fast Company. 60 July (2002): 118.

17. Buckingham, Marcus and Donald Clifton. Now, Discover Your Strengths. Toronto: Free Press, 2001.

18. Ibis.

19. Ibis.

20. Ibis.

21. Drucker, Peter. Quote on Heartmath Institute website. <www.heartmath.com> (2003).

22. Collins, Jim. "Built to Flip," Fast Company May (2002).

23. Whistler/Blackcomb. Website. <www.whistler-blackcomb.com> (2003).

24. Freeplay, Inc. Website. <www.freeplay.net> (2003).

25. Merck & Company. Website <www.merck.com> (2003).

26. Cone/Roper. "Cause-Related Trends Report: The Evolution of Cause Branding®." (1999).

27. Hirshberg, Gary. "The Art of the Deal: How Values Can Grow Your Value." Speech. Natural Business Market Trends Conference. Colorado, June (2002).

28. Robb, Walter. "Retailer Summit: The SuperNaturals." Speech. Natural Business Market Trends Conference. Colorado, June (2002).

29. Shell International. "People and Connections: Global Scenarios to 2020." Report. <www.shell.com> (2002).

30. Chereson Group. "Study of Working Adults." Report. 20 Aug (2001).

31. Tom's of Maine. "Common Good Annual Report." <www.tomsofmaine.com> (2001-2002).

32. Chappell, Tom. "Managing Upside Down." Natural Business Market Trends Conference. Colorado, June (2002).

33. Drucker, Peter. Quote in The Economist Nov (2001).

Chapter 7

1. Brown, Juanita, David Isaacs, Eric Vogt and Nancy Margulies. "Strategic Questioning: Engaging People's Best Thinking." The Systems Thinker 13:9 Nov (2002).

2. Peavey, Fran. By Life's Grace: Musings on the Essence of Social Change. New Society Publishers, 1994.

3. Winograd, Terry and Fernando Flores. Understanding Computers and Cognition: A New Foundation for Design. Norwood: Ablex Publishing Corporation, 1986.

4. De Pree, Max. Leadership is an Art. Reissued. New York: Dell Books, 1990.

5. "Americans' Confidence in Major U.S. Institutions." Report. Worthin Worldwide, July 2002.

6. Losada, Marcial and Emily Heaphy. "The Role of Positivity and Connectivity in the Performance of Business Teams: A Nonlinear Dynamics Model." Draft. Article to be published in American Behavioral Scientist Spring (2004).

7. Peavey, Fran. "Strategic Questioning: An Approach to Creating Personal and Social Change." In Context: A Quarterly for Humane Sustainable Culture 40 Spring (1995): 36.

8. Peavey, Fran. "A Strategic Questioning Toolbox." Ed. Vivian Hutchison. <www.jobsletter.org> (2002).

9. Szent-Gyorgi, Albert. Nobel Laureate of Physiology and Medicine. Acceptance Speech. 1937.

10. Porto, Kim. "Encouraging Corporate Cultural Shifts Using Cafes." <www.worldcafe.com> (2003).

11. Brown, Juanita, David Isaacs, Eric Vogt and Nancy Margulies. "Strategic Questioning: Engaging People's Best Thinking." The Systems Thinker 13:9 Nov (2002).

12. Peavey, Fran. By Life's Grace: Musings on the Essence of Social Change. New Society Publishers, 1994.

13. Salk, Jonas. "The Science of Hope with Jonas Salk." PBS Video. A World of Ideas with Bill Moyer (1990).

14. Brown, Juanita, David Isaacs, Eric Vogt and Nancy Margulies. "Strategic Questioning: Engaging People's Best Thinking." The Systems Thinker 13:9 Nov (2002).

15. Peavey, Fran. By Life's Grace: Musings on the Essence of Social Change. New Society Publishers, 1994.

16. Rilke, Rainer Maria. Letters to a Young Poet. Reissued. New York: W.W. Norton & Company, 1993.

Chapter 8

1. Taylor, Jim and Watts Wacker. The Visionary's Handbook. HarperBusiness, 2000.

2. Rinpoche, Sogyal. The Tibetan Book of Living and Dying. San Francisco: Harper, 1992.

3. Peck, M. Scott. A Road Less Traveled. Reissued. Carmichael: Touchstone Books, 2003.

4. Wackernagel, Matthis. "Framing the Sustainability Crisis: Getting from Concern to Action." Research Paper. Sustainable Development Research Initiative, Oct <www.sdri.ubc.ca> (1997).

5. Lama, The Dalai. Compassion and Competition. Rotterdam: Asoka Publishers, 2002.

6. Beck, Don and Chris Cowan. Spiral Dynamics: Mastering Values, Leadership and Change. Malden: Blackwell Publishing, 1996.

7. Einstein, Albert. Evolution of Physics. Cambridge: Cambridge University Press, 1971: 152.

8. Florida, R. The Rise of the Creative Class and How It's Transforming Work, Leisure, Community and Everyday Life. New York: Basic Books, 2002.

9. Rubin, Harriet. "Living Dangerously." Column. Fast Company. Permission for quote granted directly from author. Dec 2003.

10. Petzinger, Thomas. "A New Model for the Nature of Business: It's Alive!," Wall Street Journal. 26 Feb 1999.

11. Ibis.

12. Havel, Vaclav. "Help the Soviet Union on its Road to Democracy: Consciousness precedes Being." Address. Joint Session of Congress. Washington, D.C. 21 Feb 1990.

Appendix

1. Sakharov, Andrei. My Country and the World. New York: Knopf, 1975.

The Wisdom Underlying
The 7 Essentials^{sm}

The 7 Essentials^{sm} isn't merely intellectual theory nor is it the latest management fad. It reflects core patterns of human wisdom accumulated across Western and Eastern philosophies and sciences as well as the authors' years of practical experience facilitating the development of formal and informal leaders and groups of all shapes and sizes. Three broadly-defined fields and a few contemporary sources that the framework draws from are:

- *The dynamics of living systems*—a deep understanding about organic life and its complexities amassed by thinkers such as David Bohm, Fritjof Capra, Daniel Kaufman, Humberto Maturana, Ilya Prigogene, Karl-Henrik Robert, Mitchell Waldrop, Margaret Wheatley and Ken Wilber.

- *Human dynamics*—knowledge about how humans evolve, create health and function effectively as individuals and organizations. Among others, these authors have been invaluable resources: Chris Argyris, Don Beck, Joan Borysenko, Marcus Buckingham, Pema Chodron, Deepak Chopra, Curt Coffman, David Cooperrider, Stephen Covey, Larry Dossey, Robert Emmons, Erik Erikson, Victor Frankl, Robert Fritz, Georg Feuerstein, Howard Gardner, Daniel Goleman, Ernest Holmes, George Kelly, Fred Kofman, Harold Koenig, Peter Koestenbaum, Carl Jung, Abraham Maslow, Thomas Moore, Julio Olalla, Kenneth Pelletier, Dan Pink, Elizabeth, Kubler-Ross, Peter Russell, Sandra Seagal, Martin Seligman, Peter Senge, Robert Thurman, Francisco Varela, Jenny Wade and Ken Wilber.

- *Marketplace and business dynamics*—insights about trends in business, their effects on the marketplace and visa versa. This includes the role companies can play as positive global citizens to create sustainable economies, civilizations and business success. It also takes into account the social and consumer movements toward health and sustainability. A few of the many thinkers that have influenced us are: Warren Bennis, Lester Brown, Jim Collins, Peter Drucker, Duane Elgin, John Elkington, Richard Florida, Paul Hawkens, Hazel Henderson, Adrian Hodges, Eamonn Kelly, David Korten, Willis Harman, Barry Oshry, Jagdish Parikh, Daryl Paulson, Paul Ray, Peter Senge and Mathis Wackernagel.

We notice a common enterprise weaving through the work of many of these well-respected professionals: *the desire to architect a healthier and more inclusive understanding of reality* (albeit, each using a particular reference point to do so.) From the biological lessons of Fritjof Capra to the focused management insights of Peter Drucker to the wide-sweeping views of Ken Wilber, we sought to gain knowledge from people largely concerned with enhancing the total health and effectiveness of humankind and the planet. The evolution of *The 7 Essentials*^{sm} would not have been possible without the abundance of knowledge these thinkers and their contemporaries continue to develop and share. Drawing in part on their work as well as experiences of our own, *The 7 Essentials*^{sm} is our attempt to bring what we've learned into a coherent and concrete framework for adept leaders who want to use business as an avenue to cultivate wide-spanning, healthier forms of success.

Please browse the Bibliography to find a comprehensive list of our sources.

Bibliography

Albion, Mark. Making a Life, Making a Living. New York: Warner Business Books, 2000.

American Heritage Dictionary. Second College Edition. Boston: Houghton Mifflin Company, 1985.

"Americans' Confidence in Major U.S. Institutions." Report. Worthin Worldwide, July 2002.

Argyris, Chris. Knowledge for Action: A Guide to Overcoming Barriers to Organizational Change. San Francisco: Jossey-Bass Publishers, 1993.

——. On Organizational Learning. Malden: Blackwell Publishing, 1999.

——. Overcoming Organizational Defenses: Facilitating Organizational Learning. Needham: Allyn & Bacon, 1990.

——. "Teaching Smart People How to Learn." Harvard Business Review 69.3 (1991): 99.

Badiner, Allan Hunt. Mindfulness in the Marketplace. Berkeley: Parallax Press, 2002.

Ban Breathnack, Sarah. Simple Abundance: A Daybook of Comfort and Joy. New York: Warner Books, 1995.

Beck, Don and Chris Cowan. Spiral Dynamics: Mastering Values, Leadership and Change. Malden: Blackwell Publishing, 1996.

Belkin, Lisa. "The Opt-Out Revolution." The New York Times 26 Oct 2003.

Bennis, Warren. "Crucibles of Leadership." Harvard Business Review 80.9 (2002): 39.

——. "Five Competencies of New Leaders." Executive Excellence 16.7 (1999): 4.

——. "Leaders of Ideas." Executive Excellence 17.2 (2000): 8.

——. On Becoming a Leader: The Leadership Classic. Cambridge: Perseus Publishing, 2003.

——. Reinventing Leadership: Strategies to Empower the Organization. New York: HarperTrade, 1997.

——. "Towards a 'Truly' Scientific Moment: The Concept of Organization Health." The SOL Journal 4.1 (2002): 4.

——. Quoted in New Traditions in Business: Spirit and Leadership in the 21st Century. By John Renesch. New York: Prima Lifestyles, 1992.

Bennis, Warren, Jagdish Parikh and Ronnie Essem. Global Leadership: The Next Generation. Paramus: Financial Times/Prentice Hall, 2003.

——. Beyond Leadership: Balancing Economics, Ethics and Ecology. Cambridge: Blackwell Business, 1996.

Bohm, David. On Dialogue. New York: Routledge, 1996.

——. Thought as a System. New York: Routledge, 1994.

——. Wholeness and the Implicate Order. New York: Routledge, 2002.

Bollier, David. Silent Theft: The Plunder of Our Common Wealth. New York: Routledge, 2002.

Borysenko, Joan. Fire in the Soul: A New Psychology of Spiritual Optimism. New York: Warner Books, 1994.

——. Guilt is the Teacher, Love is the Lesson: A Book to Heal You Heart and Soul. New York: Warner Books, 1991.

——. Minding the Body, Mending the Mind. New York: Bantam Books, 1988.

Branfman, Fred. "Legacies." Imagine: What American Could be in the 21st Century. Ed. Marianne Williamson. New York: Daybreak, 2000.

Brown, Juanita, David Isaacs, Eric Vogt and Nancy Margulies. "Strategic Questioning: Engaging People's Best Thinking." The Systems Thinker 13:9 Nov (2002).

Brown, Lester. "The Eco-Economic Revolution." The Futurist 36:2 (2002): 23.

——. Eco-Economy: Building a New Economy for the Earth. New York: W.W. Norton & Company, 2001.

Buckingham, Marcus, and Curt Coffman. First, Break All the Rules: What the World's Greatest Managers Do Differently. New York: Simon & Schuster Adult Publishing Group, 1999.

Buckingham, Marcus and Donald Clifton. Now, Discover Your Strengths. Toronto: Free Press, 2001.

Buddha, Gautama. Quoted in True Work: Doing What You Love and Loving What You Do. By Michael and Justine Toms. New York: Harmony/Bell Tower, 1999.

"Business and Sustainability Development: A Global Guide." Case Study on British Petroleum. <www.bsdglobal.com> (2002).

"Business Case for Corporate Citizenship." Report. Arthur D. Little <www.adl.com> (2002).

Cairncross, Frances. "Tough at the Top." The Economist 23 Oct (2003).

Capra, Frijof. The Hidden Connections: Integrating the Biological, Cognitive and Social Dimensions of Life into a Science of Sustainability. New York: Doubleday Publishing, 2002.

——. The Turning Point. New York: Bantam Books, 1984.

——. The Web of Life: A New Understanding of Living Systems. New York: Doubleday Publishing, 1997.

Cashman, Kevin. LeaderSource, Inc. <www.leadersource.com> (2003).

Chappell, Tom. "Managing Upside Down." Natural Business Market Trends Conference. Colorado, June (2002).

Chereson Group. "Study of Working Adults." Report. 20 Aug (2001).

Chodron, Pema. Start Where You Are: A Guide to Compassionate Living. Boston: Shambhala Publications, 2001.

Chopra, Deepak. Ageless Body, Timeless Mind: The Quantum Alternative to Growing Old. New York: Random House, 1997.

——. Perfect Health: The Complete Mind Body Guide. New York: Crown Publishing Group, 2001.

——. Quoted in Making a Life, Making a Living. By Mark Albion. New York: Warner Business Books, 2000: 2.

——. Quantum Healing: Exploring the Frontiers of Mind Body Medicine. New York: Bantam Books, 1990.

——. The Seven Spiritual Laws of Success. Crown Publishing Group, 2001.

Chopra, Deepak and Candace B Pert. Molecules of Emotion: The Science behind Mind-Body Medicine. New York: Simon & Schuster Adult Publishing Group, 1999.

Chua, Amy. "Making the World Safe for Markets." Harvard Business Review. Aug (2003).

Cincotta, Richard and Robert Engelman. Nature's Place: Human Population and the Future of Biological Diversity. Population Action International, 2000.

Collins, Jim. Good to Great: Why Some Companies Make the Leap and Others Don't. New York: HarperBusiness, 2001.

—. "Built to Flip," Fast Company May (2002).

Cone/Roper. "Cause-Related Trends Report: The Evolution of Cause Branding®." (1999).

Conscious Media, Inc. "The Natural Business LOHAS Report: A Study of the Market for Lifestyles of Health and Sustainability." (2000).

Cooperrider, David. "Appreciative Inquiry Commons." Website portal for resources and tools about the application of Appreciative Inquiry. <http://connection.cwru.edu/ai/> (2003).

Cortese, Amy. "They Care About the World (and They Shop, Too)." New York Times 20 July (2003).

Covey, Stephen. Leadership. New York: Free Press, 2002.

—. Principle Centered Leadership. New York: Simon & Schuster, 1992.

—. The Seven Habits of Highly Effective People: Powerful Lessons in Personal Change. New York: Simon & Schuster, 1990.

Covey, Stephen, Rebecca Merrill and Roger A. Merrill. First Things First: To Live, to Love, to Learn, to Leave a Legacy. New York: Simon & Schuster Trade Paperbacks, 1995.

Coyote, Peter. "The Arts." Imagine: What American Could be in the 21st Century. Ed. Marianne Williamson. New York: Daybreak, 2000.

Crooke, Michael. "The Integration of Environmental Activism, Social Integrity and Healthy Financial Performance at Patagonia." Natural Business Market Trends Conference. Colorado, June (2003).

Csikszentmihalyi, Mihaly, William Damon and Howard Gardner. Good Work: When Excellence and Ethics Meet. New York: Basic Books, 2001.

CSRWire. Corporate Social Responsibility Forum for Business Leaders <CSRwire.com> (2003).

Daft, Doug. Speech. Brandeis University International Business School. 13 Nov (2003).

DeGeus, Arie, and Peter Senge. The Living Company: Growth, Learning and Longevity in Business. Boston: Harvard Business School Press, 1997.

De Pree, Max. Leadership is an Art. Reissued. New York: Dell Books, 1990.

Dossey, Larry. Beyond Illness: Discovering the Experience of Health. Boston: Shambhala Publications, 1985.

—. Beyond the Body: Medicine and the Infinite Reach of the Mind. Boston: Shambhala Publications, 2003.

—. Healing Words: The Power of Prayer and the Practice of Medicine. San Francisco: HarperSanFrancisco, 1995.

—. Recovering the Soul: A Scientific and Spiritual Approach. New York: Bantam Doubleday Dell Publishers, 1989.

—. Reinventing Medicine: Beyond Mind-Body to a New Era of Healing. San Francisco: Harper, 2000.

Drucker, Peter. Concept of the Corporation. Piscataway: Transaction Publishers, 2001.

——. "Managing Oneself." Harvard Business Review 77.2 (1999): 64.

——. Management Challenges for the 21st Century. New York: HarperInformation, 2001.

——. "Management's New Paradigms." Forbes 162.7 (1998): 152.

——. Post-Capitalist Society. New York: HarperInformation, 1999.

——. "The Discipline of Innovation." Harvard Business Review 80.8 (2002): 95.

——. The Effective Executive. New York: HarperInformation, 2002.

——. The New Realities. Piscataway: Transaction Publishers, 2003.

——. "They're Not Employees, They're People." Harvard Business Review 80.2 (2002): 70.

——. "What is Our Business?" Executive Excellence 18.6 (2001): 3.

——. Quote in The Economist. Nov (2001).

——. Quote on Heartmath Institute website. <www.heartmath.com> (2003).

——. The Post-Capitalistic Society. New York: HarperBusiness, 1993.

"Economist Reports on Corporate Leadership, Governance." Continuum 17:23 World Business Academy. 28 Oct 2003.

Eamonn, Kelly, Peter Leyden and members of the Global Business Network. What's Next: Exploring the New Terrain for Business. Cambridge: Perseus Publishing, 2002.

Einstein, Albert. "What I Believe." Forum and Century 84 (1930): 193-194.

——. Evolution of Physics. Cambridge: Cambridge University Press, 1971: 152.

——. Quoted in Quantum Reality: Beyond the New Physics. By Nick Herbert. New York: Anchor/Doubleday, 1987: 250.

Elgin, Duane. Voluntary Simplicity. New York: William Morrow: 1981.

Elgin, Duane and Coleen LeDrew. Global Consciousness Change: Indicators on an Emerging Paradigm. San Anselmo: Millennium Project <www.awakeningearth.org/reports/gcc/pdf> 1997.

Elkington, John. The Chrysalis Economy: How Citizen CEOs and Corporations Can Fuse Values and Value Creation. Hoboken: John Wiley & Sons, 2001.

Emmons, Robert. "Is Spirituality an Intelligence? Motivation, Cognition, and the Psychology of Ultimate Concern." International Journal for the Psychology of Religion 10.1 (2000): 3.

——. The Psychology of Ultimate Concerns: Motivation and Spirituality in Personality. New York: Guilford Publications, 1999.

Erikson, Erik. The Erik Erikson Reader. Ed. Robert Coles. New York: W.W. Norton & Company, 2001.

Feuerstein, Georg. Living Yoga: A Comprehensive Guide for Daily Life. New York: The Putnam Publishing Group, 1993.

——. Wholeness or Transcendence: Ancient Lessons for the Emerging Global Civilization. Burdett: Larson Publications, 1992.

——. The Yoga Tradition: History, Religion, Philosophy and Practice. Prescott: Hohm Press, 2001.

Florida, Richard. "The New American Dream." Washington Monthly 35.2 (2003): 26.

——. The Rise of the Creative Class and How It's Transforming Work, Leisure, Community and Everyday Life. New York: Basic Books, 2002.

Forrestor, Jay. Principles of Systems. Waltham: Pegasus Communications, 1968.

Frankl, Victor. Man's Search for Ultimate Meaning. Cambridge: Perseus Publishing, 2000.

Freeplay, Inc. Website. <www.freeplay.net> (2003).

Fritz, Robert. Creating. New York: Ballantine Books, 1993.

—. The Path of Least Resistance for Managers: Designing Organizations to Succeed. San Francisco: Berrett-Koehler Publishers, 1999.

—. Path of Least Resistance. New York: Ballantine Books, 1989.

Fuller, R. Buckminster with Jerome Agel and Quentin Fiore. I Seem To Be a Verb. New York: Bantam Books, 1970.

Garcia, A. "The Tao Index Rose Today…," LOHAS Journal 2:4 (2001).

Garland, Judy. Quoted in Simple Abundance: A Daybook of Comfort and Joy. Sarah Ban Breathnack. New York: Warner Books, 1995: 31.

Gardner, Howard. Frames of Mind: The Theory of Multiple Intelligences. New York: Basic Books, 1993.

—. Leading Minds: An Anatomy of Leadership. New York: Basic Books, 1996.

—. The Mind's New Science: A History of Cognitive Revolution. New York: Basic Books, 1987.

—. Multiple Intelligences: The Theory in Practice. New York: Basic Books, 1993.

Gilmartin, Ray. "Improving Access to Health Care and Medicines in a World Without Borders." World. Newsletter. Merck & Company, Aug (2002).

"Globalisation of the Organic Food Industry." Organic Monitor 14 July <www.organicmonitor. com> (2003).

Goleman, Daniel. Emotional Intelligence. New York: Bantam Books, 1996.

—. Emotional Intelligence: Why It Can Matter More than IQ. New York: Bantam Books, 1997.

Grayson, David and Adrian Hodges. Everybody's Business: Managing Risks and Opportunities in Today's Global Society. London: Dorling Kindserley Press, 2002.

Greider, William. The Soul of Capitalism: Opening Paths to a Moral Economy. New York: Simon & Schuster, 2003.

Hansen, Mark and Robert Allen. The One Minute Millionaire. New York: Harmony Books, 2002.

Harman, Willis. Global Mind Change: The Promise of the 21st Century. San Francisco: Berrett-Koehler Publishers, 1998.

Harman, Willis, John Hormann and Stan Janger. Creative Work: The Constructive Role of Business in a Transforming Society. Indianapolis: Knowledge Systems, 1990.

Hartman, H. Marketing in the Soul Age: Building Lifestyle Worlds. Bellevue: The Hartman Group, 2001.

Havel, Vaclav. "Help the Soviet Union on its Road to Democrary: Consciousness precedes Being." Address. Joint Session of Congress. Washington, D.C. 21 Feb 1990.

Hawken, Paul. The Ecology of Commerce: A Declaration of Sustainability. New York: Harper Business, 1994.

—. Growing a Business. New York: Simon & Schuster, 1987.

Hawken, Paul, Amory Lovins and Hunter L. Lovins. Natural Capitalism: Creating the Next Industrial Revolution. Boston: Little, Brown & Company, 2000.

Hawley, H. "Surveying Corporate Environmental and Social Reporting," The Ethical Corporation Magazine Feb (2002).

HeartMath Institute. <www.heartmath.com> (2003).

Henderson, Hazel. Beyond Globalization: Shaping a Sustainable Global Economy. Bloomfield: Kumarian Press, 1999.

——. "Brasil: Key Player in a New World Game," Signposts 17:1 Feb 26 (2003).

——. Building a Win-Win World: Life Beyond Global Economic Warfare. San Francisco: Berrett-Koehler Publishers, 1996.

——. Paradigms in Progress: Life Beyond Economics. San Francisco: Berrett-Koehler Publishers, 1995.

Herbert, Nick. Quantum Reality: Beyond the New Physics. New York: Anchor/Doubleday, 1987.

Hirshberg, Gary. "The Art of the Deal: How Values Can Grow Your Value." Speech. Natural Business Market Trends Conference. Colorado, June (2002).

Holliday, C. "Sustainable Growth, the DuPont Way." Harvard Business Review Sept (2001).

Holmes, Ernest. Science of Mind. New York: The Putnam Publishing Group, 1997.

——. This Thing Called Life. New York: The Putnam Publishing Group, 1997.

——. Living the Science of Mind. Eighth Edition. Marina del Ray: DeVorss & Company, 1999.

Horne, David and Sandra Seagal. Human Dynamics: A New Framework for Understanding People and Realizing the Potential in Our Organizations. Waltham: Pegasus Communications, 1997.

Hutchens, David. The Lemming Dilemma. Pegasus Communications, Boston, 2000.

IMF World Economic Outlook. Report. April <www.imf.org> (2003).

Inayat Khan, Hazrat . The Art of Being and Becoming. (originally published as Personality: The Art of Being and Becoming) New Lebanon: Omega Publications, 1990.

Innovation Associates. Systems Thinking Curriculum (1997).

Jung, Carl. The Archetypes and The Collective Unconscious. Collected Works of C.G. Jung Vol. 9 Part 1. Ed. Michael Fordham and R.F.C. Hull. Princeton: Princeton University Press, 1981.

——. The Four Basic Psychological Functions of Man and the Establishment of Uniformities in Human Structures and Human Behavior. Albuquerque: The American Institute for Psychological Research, 1984.

——. Man and His Symbols. New York: Dell Publishing, 1968.

——. Memories, Dreams, Reflections. Ed. Aniela Jaffe. New York: Vintage Books, 1989.

Kaufman, Daniel. Corporate Partnering: Structuring and Negotiating Domestic and International Strategic Alliances. Gaithersburg: Aspen Publishers, 1994.

——. To Be a Man: Visions of Self, Views from Within. New York: Simon & Schuster Adult Publishing Group, 1994.

Kauffman, Draper. Systems 1: An Introduction to Systems Thinking. Future Systems, 1980.

Kellner-Rogers, Myron, and Margaret Wheatley. A Simpler Way. San Francisco: Berrett-Koehler Publishers, 1996.

Kelly, George. The Psychology of Personal Constructs. New York: Routledge, 1992.

—. The Psychology of Constructs. Vol. 2. New York: Routledge, 1992.

Kelly, Marjorie. The Divine Right of Capital. San Francisco: Berrett-Koehler, 2001.

Kennedy, Ellen. "The LOHAS Advantage." Presentation. The Natural Market Trends LOHAS Conference. Colorado, 18 June 2003.

Kiley, David. "Zingerman's Took the Road Less Traveled to Success." USA Today Wed 1 Oct (2003).

Kramer, Robert. "The Harder They Fall." Harvard Business Review 81:10 Oct (2003).

Koenig, Harold. Handbook of Religion and Health: A Century of Research Reviewed. New York: Oxford University Press, 2001.

—. Is Religion Good for Your Health? The Effects of Religion on Physical and Mental Health. Binghamton: The Haworth Press, 1997.

Koestenbaum, Peter. "Koestenbaum's Weekly Leadership Thought." Newsletter. 15 July 2002.

—. Leadership: The Inner Side of Greatness: A Philosophy for Leaders, New and Revised. Hoboken: John Wiley & Sons, 2002.

—. The Heart of Business. Dallas: Saybrook Publishing, 1991.

Koestenbaum, Peter and Peter Block. Freedom and Accountability at Work: Applying Philosophic Insight to the Real World. Hoboken: John Wiley & Sons, 2001.

Kofman, Fred, and Peter M. Senge. "Communities of Commitment: The Heart of Learning Organizations." Organizational Dynamics 22:2 (1993).

Korten, David. "The Post-Corporate World." Yes! A Journal of Positive Futures (2002). Reprinted as "Local Living Economies vs. The Suicide Economy," In Business Jul/Aug (2002).

—. The Post-Corporate World, Life After Capitalism. San Francisco: Berrett-Koehler Publishers, 2001.

—. When Corporations Rule the World. Bloomfield: Kumarian Press, 2000.

Kubler-Ross, Elizabeth and Kenneth Ring. Heading Toward Omega: In Search of the Meaning of the Near-Death Experience. New York: HarperTrade, 1985.

Lama, The Dalai. Compassion and Competition. Rotterdam: Asoka Publishers, 2002.

Lampe, Frank and Steve French. "LOHAS Consumer Migration Patterns." LOHAS Journal Summer (2002).

Lear, Norman. Chairman and CEO, Act III Communications and Founder of Business Enterprise Trust. Quoted at <www.davender.com> (2003).

Leeds, Dorothy. "The Power of Questions." Training & Development 54:10 Oct (2000): 20.

Lerner, Michael. Spirit Matters. Charlottesville: Walsh Books, Hampton Roads Publishing Company, 2000.

Losada, Marcial and Emily Heaphy. "The Role of Positivity and Connectivity in the Performance of Business Teams: A Nonlinear Dynamics Model." Draft. Article to be published in American Behavioral Scientist Spring (2004).

Manga, Manuel. "The Evolutionary Leader of the Future: A New Observer and Designer of Organizations and Social Systems." Center for Evolutionary Leadership. Report. <www.wfs.org> (2002).

Marketing Intelligence Service, Ltd. "Build a Better Mousetrap: 2002 New Product Innovations of the Year." (2002).

Maslow, Abraham. Maslow on Management. Hoboken: John Wiley & Sons, 1998.

—-. The Farther Reaches of Human Nature. New York: Penguin Putnam, 1993.

—-. Toward a Psychology of Being. Hoboken: John Wiley & Sons, 1998.

Master's Study Bible. Nashville: Holman Bible Publishers, 1981.

Maturana, Humberto and Francisco Varela. The Tree of Knowledge: The Biological Roots of Human Understanding. Boston: Shambhala Publications, 1988.

McDonough, William and Michael Braungart. Cradle to Cradle. New York: North Point Press, 2002.

McGreal, Ian. Great Thinkers of the Eastern World. New York: HarperCollins Publishing, 1995.

Meadows, Donella. "Which Future?" In Context: A Quarterly of Humane Sustainable Culture 43 Winter (1995-96).

Meadows, Donella, Dennis Meadows and Jörgen Randers. Beyond the Limits. Toronto: McClelland & Stewart, 1992.

Merck & Company. Website <www.merck.com> (2003).

"Merck Earns Highest Rating in Ethics Study." About Merck <www.merck.com> (2003).

Merton, Thomas. Seeds. Ed. Robert Inchausti. Boston: Shambhala, 2002.

Moore, Thomas. Care of the Soul: A Guide for Cultivating Depth and Sacredness in Everyday Life. New York: Perennial Publishers, 1994.

Moorefield, Kathleen Renee. An Innovative Look at Spirituality and Personality. Dissertation. Greenwich University (2002).

Morse, Gardiner. "Bottom-Up Economics." Harvard Business Review Aug (2003): 18-20.

Nattrass, Brian and Mary Altomare. Dancing with the Tiger. Canada: New Society Publishers, 2002.

—-. The Natural Step for Business. BC: New Society Publishers, 2001: 13-14.

Natural Marketing Institute. "Understanding the LOHAS Consumer Report.™" (2003).

Neal, J.A. "Work as Service to the Divine," American Behavioral Scientist 43 (2000): 8.

Nussbaum, Barbara. "Ubuntu and Business ... Reflections and Questions." Perspectives 17:3 7 May (2003).

Nussbaum, Martha. Quoted in article by Harriet Rubin. "Global Values in a Local World." Fast Company 60 July (2002).

Nutt, Paul. Why Decisions Fail. San Francisco: Berrett Koehler, 2002.

O'Brien, William. The Soul of Corporate Leadership. Innovations in Management Series. Waltham: Pegasus Communications, 1998.

Olalla, Julio and Rafael Echeverria. "Management by Coaching." HR Focus 73.1 (1996): 16.

Orstein, Robert and Paul Ehrlich. New World, New Mind: Moving Toward Conscious Evolution. New York: Doubleday, 1989.

Oshry, Barry. Seeing Systems: Unlocking the Mysteries of Organizational Life. San Francisco: Berrett-Koehler Publishers, 1996.

O'Sullivan, Kate. "Strategies: The Don't-Take-It-to-Market Alternative," Inc. Magazine Dec (2002).

Parikh, Jagdish, Franz F. Neubauer and Alden G. Lank. Intuition: The New Frontier of Management. Malden: Blackwell Publishing, 1994.

—. Managing Relationships: Making a Life While Making a Living. Hoboken: John Wiley & Sons, 2001.

—. Managing Your Self: Management by Detached Involvement. Malden: Blackwell Publishing, 1991.

Paulson, Daryl. "The Hard Issues of Life." Pastoral Psychology 49.5 (2001): 385.

Paulson, Daryl and Ken Wilber. Competitive Business, Caring Business: An Integral Business Perspective for the 21st Century. New York: Paraview Press, 2002.

Payutto, Ven. P.A. "Buddhist Perspectives on Economic Concepts." Mindfulness in the Marketplace. Ed. Allan Hunt Badiner. Berkeley: Pallalax Press, 2002.

Peavey, Fran. "A Strategic Questioning Toolbox." Ed. Vivian Hutchison. <www.jobsletter.org> (2002).

—. By Life's Grace: Musings on the Essence of Social Change. New Society Publishers, 1994.

—. "Strategic Questioning," CDRA Nugget Feb (2002). <www.crda.org>.

—. "Strategic Questioning: An Approach to Creating Personal and Social Change." In Context: A Quarterly for Humane Sustainable Culture 40 Spring (1995): 36.

Peck, M. Scott. A Road Less Traveled. Reissued. Carmichael: Touchstone Books, 2003

Pelletier, Kenneth. Healthy People in Unhealthy Places: Stress and Fitness at Work. New York: Dell Publishing, 1984.

—. Sound Mind, Sound Body: A New Model For Lifelong Health. New York: Simon & Schuster Adult Publishing Group, 1994.

Petzinger, Thomas. "A New Model for the Nature of Business: It's Alive!," Wall Street Journal. 26 Feb 1999.

"Pick Your Poison: NC Exec Struggles to do the Right Thing." Continuum 17:23 World Business Academy. 29 Oct (2003).

Pink, Dan. Free Agent Nation. New York: Warner Books, 2001.

Porto, Kim. "Encouraging Corporate Cultural Shifts Using Cafes." <www.worldcafe.com> (2003).

Post, S.G. Altruism and Altruistic Love: Science, Philosophy, and Religion in Dialogue. Introduction. Ed. Post, S.G., et al. New York: Oxford University Press, 2002.

Pralahad, C.K. Quote from <www.edgewalkers.com> (2003).

Preston, Lynelle. "Sustainability at Hewlett-Packard: From Theory to Practice." California Management Review 43:3 Spring (2001).

Prigogene, Ilya. Order Out of Chaos. New York: Bantam Books, 1983.

—. Self-Organization in Nonequilibrium Systems: From Dissipative Structures to Order through Fluctuations. New York: John Wiley & Sons, 1977.

Quidar, Iqbal. "Bottom-Up Economics." Harvard Business Review Aug (2003).

Ray, Paul. "LOHAS and the Emerging Economy: Structural Changes." LOHAS Conference. Colorado, June (2003).

—. "Modernists and Heartlanders." American Demographics 19.2 (1997): 33.

—. "The Emerging Culture." American Demographics 19.2 (1997): 29.

—. The New Political Compass. Version 7.3, © Paul Ray, April 2002.

Ray, Paul and Sherry Ruth Anderson. The Cultural Creatives: How 50 Million People are Changing the World. New York: Crown Publishing Group, 2000.

Reder, A. Best Business Practices for Socially Responsible Companies. New York: Tarcher/Putnam, 1995.

Renesch, John. New Traditions in Business: Spirit and Leadership in the 21st Century. New York: Prima Lifestyles, 1992.

Reputation and Risk. General Report. CSRWire. Corporate Social Responsibility Forum for Business Leaders <CSRwire.com> (1998).

Rilke, Rainer Maria. Letters to a Young Poet. Reissued. New York: W.W. Norton & Company, 1993.

Rinpoche, Sogyal. The Tibetan Book of Living and Dying. San Francisco: Harper, 1992.

Robb, Walter. "Retailer Summit: The SuperNaturals." Speech. Natural Business Market Trends Conference. Colorado, June (2002).

Robert, Karl-Henrik. The Natural Step: The Seeding of a Quiet Revolution. Gabriola Island: New Society Publishers, 2002.

Robinson, Vicki. "From 'Excess' to 'Enough'—Shifting the Culture of Consumption." Report. Seattle: The New Road Map Foundation, <www.newroadmap.org> 1996.

Roddick, Anita. "The Revolutionary Eccentric." Hope Jul/Aug 38 (2003) 12.

Roof, W.C. Spiritual Marketplace. Princeton: Princeton University Press, 1997.

Rosch, Eleanor, Evan Thompson and Francisco Varela. The Embodied Mind: Cognitive Science and the Human Experience. Cambridge: MIT Press, 1991.

Rubin, Harriet. "Living Dangerously." Column. Fast Company. Permission for quote granted directly from author. Dec 2003.

—. "Global Values in a Local World," Fast Company 60 July (2002).

Russell, Peter. The Global Brain Awakens: Our Next Evolutionary Leap. Boston: Element Books, 2000.

—. Waking Up in Time: Finding Inner Peace in Times of Accelerating Change. Novato: Origin Press, 1998.

Sakharov, Andrei. My Country and the World. New York: Knopf, 1975.

Salk, Jonas. "The Science of Hope with Jonas Salk." PBS Video. A World of Ideas with Bill Moyer (1990).

Saloff-Coste, M. "Strategies of the Future." Perspectives 15:5. World Business Academy. 19 Dec (2001).

Sanger, David and Richard Oppell. "Senate Unanimously Passes Corporate Reform Measure." New York Times 16 July 2002.

Schneider, Michael. A Beginner's Guide to Constructing the Universe: The Mathematical Archetypes of Nature, Art and Science. New York: Harper Perennial, 1995.

Schuster, J. "Wholistic Care: Healing a Sick System." Nursing Management 28(1997): 6.

Scott, Mary and Howard Rothman. Companies with a Conscience. Secaucus: Carol Publishing Group, 1994.

Seligman, Martin. Learned Optimism: How to Change Your Mind and Your Life. New York: Free Press, 1998.

—. What You Can Change and What You Can't. New York: Ballantine Books, 1995.

Senge, Peter. "Creative Tension." Executive Excellence 16.1 (1999): 12.

—. "Team Learning." McKinsey Quarterly 2 (1991): 82.

—. The Fifth Discipline Fieldbook. New York: Doubleday Publishing, 1994.

—. The Fifth Discipline: The Art and Practice of the Learning Organization. New York: Doubleday Publishing, 1995.

Senge, Peter, Art Kleiner, Charlotte Roberts, Richard Ross, George Roth and Bryan Smith. The Dance of Change: The Challenges of Sustaining Momentum in Learning. New York: Doubleday Publishing, 1999.

Shapiro, Stewart and Mark Spence. "Managerial Intuition: A Conceptual and Operational Framework," Business Horizons Jan-Feb (1997).

Sheehan, George. "Why Do I Run?" Runner's World Dec (2003): 61.

Shell International. "People and Connections: Global Scenarios to 2020." Report. <www.shell.com> (2002).

Silicon Valley Toxics Coalition. "Poison PCs/Toxic TVs." Report. <www.svtc.org> (2003).

Simonetta, Joe. "The Bottom Line." ViewPoint Newsletter. World Business Academy (2002).

Stahura, B. "Radical Ethics." Science of Mind March 2003.

Stigson, Bjorn. "Walking the Talk—The Business Case for Sustainable Development." Conference. World Business Council for Sustainable Development. 7 May (2003).

Szent-Gyorgi, Albert. Nobel Laureate of Physiology and Medicine. Acceptance Speech. 1937.

Taylor, Jim and Watts Wacker. The Visionary's Handbook. HarperBusiness, 2000.

The Byrds. Turn! Turn! Turn!. 1966 Song. Lyrics. <www.lyrics.com> (2003).

Thurman, Robert A.F. "Boardroom Buddhism." Civilization 6.6 (2000): 61.

—. Inner Revolution: Life, Liberty, and the Pursuit of Real Happiness. New York: Berkley Publishing Group, 1999.

—. "What Good is Meditation." Civilization 6.6 (2000): 59.

Tomkins, Richard. "How to Be Happy." Financial Times Mar 7 <www.ft.com> (2003).

Tom's of Maine. "Common Good Annual Report." <www.tomsofmaine.com> (2001-2002).

Toms, Michael and Justine Toms. True Work: Doing What You Love and Loving What You Do. New York: Harmony/Bell Tower, 1999.

Tonkin, Alan. "ValueNews." Newsletter. 43 Feb 23 (2003).

Tyson, Laura. "The New Economy is Dead. Long Live the New Economy." Essay. World Economic Forum Annual Meeting. (2003).

Underwood, R. "Radicals for Responsibility." Fast Company May (2002).

United Nations. Website <www.unog.ch> (2003).

Varela, Francisco. Ethical Know-How: Action, Wisdom & Cognition. Stanford: Stanford University Press, 1999.

Visions of a Better World. Peace Messenger Initiative of the United Nations. Eds. Jagdish Chander Hassija and Mohini Panjabi. The Brahma Kumaris World Spiritual University, 1994.

Wackernagel, Matthis. "Framing the Sustainability Crisis: Getting from Concern to Action." Research paper. Sustainable Development Research Initiative, <www.sdri.ubc.ca> Oct (1997).

Wade, Jenny. Changes of Mind: A Holonomic Theory of the Evolution of Consciousness. Suny Series in the Philosophy of Psychology. Albany: State University of New York Press, 1996.

Waldrop, Mitchell. Complexity: The Emerging Science at the Edge of Chaos and Order. New York: Simon & Schuster, 1992.

Wal-Mart. Website. <www.walmartstores.com> (2003).

Wheatley, Margaret. Leadership and the New Science: Discovering Order in a Chaotic World. San Francisco: Berrett-Koehler Publishers, 1999.

—. Leadership and the New Science: Learning about Organization from an Orderly Universe. San Francisco: Berrett-Koehler Publishers, 1992.

—. Turning to One Another: Simple Conversations to Return Hope to the Future. San Francisco: Berrett-Koehler, 2002.

Whistler/Blackcomb. Website. <www.whistler-blackcomb.com> (2003).

Wilber, Ken. A Brief History of Everything. Boston: Shambhala Publications, 2000.

—. A Theory of Everything, an Integral Vision for Business, Politics, Science and Spirituality. Boston: Shambhala Publications, 2001.

—. Excerpt B: The Many Ways We Touch—Three Principles. Report. (2002).

—. Integral Psychology: Consciousness, Spirit, Psychology, Therapy. Boston: Shambhala Publications, 2000.

—. Sex, Ecology, Spirituality: The Spirit of Evolution. Boston: Shambhala Publications, 2000.

Winograd, Terry and Fernando Flores. Understanding Computers and Cognition: A New Foundation for Design. Norwood: Ablex Publishing Corporation, 1986.

World Business Council for Sustainable Development. "Exploring Sustainable Development." Report. (1997).

World Economic Forum. Website <www.wef.org> (2003).

—. Corporate Responsibility Story about The Coca-Cola Company (2003).

—. Harvard Study of Stakeholder Balanced Companies (2003).

—. "Report on the 1999 Central and Eastern European Economic Summit: Shaping Europe 2000." Salzburg, Austria. 30 Jun—2 Jul (1999).

World Health Organization. "The World Health Report 2002: Reducing Risks, Promoting Healthy Life." (2002).

World Messenger. Website. <www.worldmessenger.com> (2003).

Worldwatch Institute. State of the World 2001: A Worldwatch Institute Report on Progress Toward a Sustainable Society. Toronto: Earthscan Canada, 2001.

—. State of the World 2002. Ed. Linda Starke. New York: W.W. Norton & Company, 2002.

—. Vital Signs: The Environmental Trends that are Shaping Our Future 2000. New York: W.W. Norton & Company, 2000.

—. Vital Signs 2002. New York: W.W. Norton & Company, 2002.

—. "World's Biggest Consumers Hold New Hope for Environment." Report. 24 July 2003.

Wellth Productions
Company Information

Wellth Productions advances the values and practices of health, effective performance and sustainability through products that assist 21st century leaders, practitioners and businesses.

We partner with our sister company, Wisdom Works. Wisdom Works uses the services of keynote speaking, thought partnering, training, action learning and executive coaching to support clients in generating a healthy profit, healthy people and a healthy world.

Together, *Wellth Productions* and *Wisdom Works* enable leaders to make better decisions in every moment, every day.

Better decisions include the capabilities of leaders to:

- Operate from their deepest purpose, values and strengths

- Envision healthier, more sustainable futures

- Prioritize efforts that generate the greatest benefit for the greatest span

- Influence and work with (instead of against) the nature and intelligence of living systems

- Foster the kind of thinking that produces a higher quality of behavior and results

- Ask strategic questions that open up new paths of innovation and action

- Design and learn from experiments that haven't been tried before

- Make more powerful choices for effective, responsible, wellth-driven results in life and work

The combined strengths of *Wellth Productions* and *Wisdoms Works* include:

- Expertise about the large and growing population of consumers, professionals and companies creating profitable markets for healthy products and services plus responsible ways doing business

- A proprietary, systems-based model—*The 7 Essentials*[sm]—that enables leaders and companies to effectively deal with the complexity of markets and organizations, and to make powerful decisions that benefit business and society

- Proven products, programs, services and a network of professional coaches, consultants and trainers which grow repeatable capabilities in leaders and organizations to deliver both financial wealth and social well-being

Our collaborative work is also provided through *services-in-care* to targeted non-profit activities. Currently, we focus our efforts on developing the next generation of 21st century women leaders. We believe that women leaders are increasingly aligned with the values of health and sustainability; women leaders play progressively larger roles in business, politics, education and almost every other arena of society; and, women leaders are a tipping point for positive, worldwide change.

For more information about Wellth Productions and Wisdom Works, please contact:

Wellth Productions
www.wellthproductions.com

Wisdom Works, Inc.
www.wisdom-works.net

Plus, you can find additional information about Driven by Wellth at:

www.drivenbywellth.com

Index